T0123203

Homegrown

Surviving Abuse to Live

Phasia

authorHOUSE®

AuthorHouse™
1663 Liberty Drive
Bloomington, IN 47403
www.authorhouse.com
Phone: 1 (800) 839-8640

Published by AuthorHouse 05/05/2017

ISBN: 978-1-5246-9022-9 (sc)
ISBN: 978-1-5246-9021-2 (e)

Print information available on the last page.

Homegrown . . .

✎ [1]*Jesus Kept Me*
(5/3/03 – 7:41pm & 5/4/03 – 4:52am)

I am . . .

Better . . . not bitter – for I am blessed

Crumpled . . . but not crushed – for I have covenant

Delivered . . . instead of destroyed – for I shall be disciplined

> *Jesus kept me . . .*

> *Jesus kept me.*

Everlasting . . . Eternal . . . Everything to me is who God is

Empty me of me I cry . . . Be in me and fill me with thee

Faithful . . . Forever . . . Father of the entire world I see

God is Holiness . . . indescribable by words

Justified by the King keeping His covenant of Love . . .

leaving me at a loss for words

Majesty . . . Mighty . . . Marvelous is who God is to me

> *Jesus keeps me . . .*

> *Jesus shall continue to keep me . . . in spite of me, eternally.*

---

[1] *History: The Poetic Tapestry of My Life (vol2)®. Copyright © 2004 Phasia*

[2] *History: My Story - His Glory (vol1)®. Copyright © 2003 Phasia*

Homegrown Weed . . .

This book is the result of a pregnancy. It's the seed conceived from a dream – a dream to be free from my past. Before it could be birthed, it witnessed many abortions. The most important one – was that of my "old" man. This writing is the "after birth" of all that's come before. This has been a necessary process that's allowed me to carry to full term the "new spirit" now dwelling within me. From within the secret passages of my spirit, this "new birth" is the result of long-ago memories that were once wrapped around my heart like a toxic umbilical cord. They are memories that have cried out from the open graves of my past, from the memories of my heart. That is until The Gardener, Jehovah Shalom, came and rooted out all of the old memories from my mind – the homegrown weeds – that have tried to choke and kill all the hopes and visions of my future. This is not being written to accuse or to condemn any person from my past... or in my future. It is being written to free them – and me. I'm not trying to hurt those who hurt me; I'm trying to forgive them – and myself. I've discovered the true love of God and His power rests in Love. Right now His Love is pruning and cutting away the wild growth of sin from my past, freeing up my mind. His tender care is allowing me to grow into the beautiful flower that brings smiles to the hearts of those who need comforting – who need to know they're loved. I am becoming the one He has designed me to be – before the beginning of time.

At the time I sat down at my computer and began writing this book, I couldn't claim the fame or fortune of a Bishop George L. Davis, a Bishop T.D. Jakes, a Joyce Meyer, an Israel Houghton, a Donnie McClurkin, a Bishop Keith A. Butler, or even an Oprah Winfrey. However, I can claim that I have planted inside of me the same seed of purpose that lives and produces God-like results of prosperity in their lives. Through this painful and sometimes self-destructive process of seeding and weeding in my life, I've been learning first-hand how I must reach for the sun (God's Son), so that I may truly experience the *joy* that is my covenant right as a child of God. I've been learning that like the simple "flower" of the fields, I must first burst free from my covering of dirt (those clinging sins) tossed onto my life up to this point – by others and myself. It's been a lifetime process that has brought me to see 50 years – my Jubilee season.

I have finally burst free, and I am in the midst of my purpose and ready to fulfill the call of God (Philippians 1:6 "Be The You God Created – Be Yourself") was always quoted to me by Dr. Myles Monroe. He left behind a legacy I've adopted from a final message he gave on air November 12, 2014, where he said the following: *Prioritize* (Design and Document Your Life Dreams); *Organize* (Say "No" to good, not right things in your life. Purpose is your work. Your work is different from your job, your job is your employment, your work is your gift or your deployment); and *Discipline* (Don't add your gifts to the cemetery. Die empty, like Jesus saying, "It is finished.").

We are all seeded to succeed. We are all equipped with God's greatness, a spirit of Shalom He has already planted deep on the inside of us. And by taking time and tending to God's Word, we're allowing God's hand to nurture us into greatness until we too become His history makers.

Over 44 years ago . . .

I was six, I think, when it first started happening. The *"night visits"*. They became rituals I didn't look forward to when I went to bed at night. They were the dark secrets hidden away and festering from the light of day. I thought the rituals were normal. I thought they were true expressions of love. I didn't know they were wrong in the eyes of man and God. I didn't think it was molestation or child abuse – until later.

Just like dark, dusty secrets, these rituals hid in a closet of my childhood, hoping no one would ever turn on the lights of responsibility to reveal their nastiness. The fumbling and poking became unwelcome and painful intrusions every night – into my soul, into my body, into my dreams. I was told it was "our little secret" so I would just obediently lay there trying to be quiet and trying not to fight him off. Why? Why didn't I fight, you may wonder. At first the attention made me feel special and loved. In my eagerness to please him, I started trying to accommodate his adult invasions into my childish world. It's as if I would unconsciously look forward to his visits because every child wants to be able to keep a secret and make their "step-daddy" proud of them. Even though he wasn't my biological father, he was the only man I'd ever known to be there in the home with my mother and her children. However, much later, it made me feel dirty and ashamed and angry. It cheapened who I thought I was. I remember at times, I would pretend to be deep asleep so he would become frustrated and just give up and leave the bedroom I shared with my little brother and older sister. If he tried to re-arrange my body to accommodate him, I would start to toss and turn as though I was having a bad dream, thwarting his every effort, and threatening to awake my sleeping siblings. At those times he would try to wake me by whispering commands or calling my name, before he would finally leave me alone in disappointment.

Later, I came to understand that those 'night visits' were wrong. When the rumors in our neighborhood started circulating, I felt like I was a "bad" little girl; like I had invited his attention by not refusing it. Worse, I felt abandoned by my mother. Most of all, I felt left all alone or abandoned by all the *men* I called "Daddy", my maternal grandfather and my real biological father. I hadn't seen or been around any really strong female role models in my life up to this point. I didn't know much at the time about the God my grandmother called Father, I do remember asking myself later, "Why didn't anyone love me?"

"Where were my protectors?"

"Where were they?"

"Why did they let this happen to me?" Those are questions I would ask myself over and over after each "episode," but at the time I never heard any clear reply to any of my questions.

✐ ²*Questions to Ask Yourself*
(01/31/99 - 10:30pm)

***Why do we** share painful experiences?*
Why do we ask questions that have no rational answers?

---

²·⁾   *History: My Story - His Glory (vol1)®. Copyright © 2003 Phasia*

Why do we seek fulfillment in man instead of God?
Why do we *search for love and believe someone*
cares by the level of pain they inflict?
Why do we blind ourselves to God's blessings by
focusing upon our needy circumstances?
Why do we forget we are children of God who
must nourish the Spirit and not the flesh?
Do we know *what good are regrets*
in a life that's been spent?
Do we know what good are promises that are
not a part of our Godly Covenant?
Do we know what good is love that is not heaven sent?
What good are these . . . without God?

As I revisit all of these memories, I still feel deep stirrings of anger, impotence and disappointment: Anger towards myself, for actually seeming to enjoy what had been happening to me at the time; Impotence for not being able to stop the abuse - the rape of my innocence – sooner; and Disappointment towards my mother for appearing to be so detached and even unaware of what was happening to her two little girls. "Didn't she know that her lover molested us nightly right under her nose?"

For a time, I even felt a love-hate towards him, for violating my dreams and my person. Hate for his actions against us – actions that showed his disrespect and lack of honor for our mother. Love for his being there when our own natural fathers willingly excused themselves from our lives. So you may be asking yourself, "What actually happened? How did you survive? Did you really get away from your past completely unscathed? Where are your scars? Why tell this story now? Aren't there others who will "reap the wind" from these revelations?"

There are many questions and a multitude of answers.

However, here is the sticking point for me in this review of my dark closet memories: Like a monster, my past keeps trying to resurrect itself on one hand (through familiar sexual sins) or my past is trys to drag me back down into the grave on the other hand (through rare health issues). I shall not let that be. I am covered by the Blood of Jesus, and I know the plan of the devil – the original thief and liar. It is to kill, to steal and to destroy. The Word of God clearly outlines the plan of the enemy in John 10:10 (King James Version).

> *The thief cometh not, but for to **steal**, and to **kill**,
> and to **destroy**: I am come that they might have life,
> and that they might have it more abundantly.*

I also know the plans and thoughts of God as outlined in Jeremiah 29:11 (King James Version). I am learning I am a history maker in God's mind.

> ***For I know the thoughts that I think toward
> you, saith the LORD**, thoughts of peace, and
> not of evil, to give you an expected end.*

The truth is, God works through our weaknesses when we yield ourselves to Him. This truth has been proven as God's grace has risen up and allowed me an avenue of escape from the devil's plan. He has shown HIS favor in my life in the midst of many incidents that could have proven to be deadly to my life. I know that my God keeps me from all harm – and the God of Hosts or Jehovah Tsaba – my Father alone has brought me too far for *me* to let go of His Word. He alone has promised never to leave me or to forsake me. I believe His promise. I believe His Word.

I am not writing this to "point the finger" of blame at

anyone. I understand now the ways of spiritual warfare. I know that the enemy seeks to kill, to steal, and to destroy God's anointed ones... sometimes through other people and usually through those we love the most.

We are hard pressed on every side, yet not crushed;
we are perplexed, but not in despair; persecuted, but
not forsaken; struck down, but not destroyed.
~2 Corinthians 4:8,9 (King James Version) ~

Momma died one week after my 38ᵗʰ birthday. She was 53. God I miss her so much. I never doubted she loved us. She just didn't know how to protect us. She didn't even have the power to protect herself from the abuse. We were all victims. May God bless her eternal soul; she's no longer here to fight this life's earthly battles, but we are still here. We are her legacy.

So I know that as demons keep trying to drag us down by using old strongholds and weaknesses developed from our past – they do this because we've given them these tools from our past to use as weapons against us. Satan tries to gain *toeholds* into our lives each day by encouraging us to compromise. Sometimes the enemy uses things or circumstances to pressure us to stop believing in "God" for the small yet "good" things His Word promises to manifest in our lives. Then if we allow that the enemy plants a *foothold*, by trying to direct us away from God's plans and the purposes He has for us. Each tiny step by the enemy we allow in our lives eventually turns into giant footprints that finally become varied *generational strongholds* that the enemy has hold over us.

✐ ³*A Toehold, A Foothold, A Stronghold*
(10/17/03 – 6:06pm)

~

Give Satan an inch and he'll manage to grab onto a toehold
He knows your weaknesses and if allowed will gain a foothold
Each habit not cast down and destroyed
quickly becomes a stronghold

~

Stand still and hold to your faith, trusting
God when things get tight
Watch and pray always, seeking God's
peace in your darkest night
Slow down and obey God, knowing it's
by perseverance you win this fight
If we are aware of the enemy's old and tired
tricks, his works shall not prosper in our life.

I am writing this because I need the cleansing and the healing that it shall provide and I need to be obedient to allow myself to free up others from their prisons of fear and hatred and self-disgust. I need the words to come up out of my heart, so the poison can be purged from my soul. I need to create a fresh and new memory book that has no demons; free from monsters or hidden things that try to come out to hurt the innocent heart. I need it so I can relax in the wisdom of God and be covered by His Love. I need to free myself from old memories so I don't have to hide in closets anymore. I'm also

---

3

writing this because I need to share a "way of escape" for those of you who were "led," either by curiosity or for some other reason, to pick up this book and read it. For this reason, I'm telling you my life story and like laundry I'm turning all the dirty secrets inside out – and hanging them out to air. So there'll be no more closet doors for me to hide my weaknesses behind – but with this freedom from my past, there will now be a cleansing sheet of protection I can wrap around me. I'm writing this book so that you too can finally be free.

Please forgive me (all of you Mothers, sis'tahs, Fathers, bro'thas and grandparents too) if I hurt you with this truth about molestation. I've decided to stop lugging around the funk of what's been dead (but not buried) from one relationship . . . to another . . . to another one.

Finally, please forgive me my one-time Stepfather – for I have forgiven you. If you are reading this book, I believe it is by the Holy Spirit's unction. I truly believe there is a soul-connection between my childhood abuse and the abuse I believe you once suffered in your childhood. The seeds planted have manifested bringing us full cycle. This time I'm not going to apologize for this closure. I need it to go forward. I know that God has blessed me, so I will no longer hide what happened to me in my ignorance. It will no longer leave my heart (and my soul) abnormally twisted to believe the wrong definition of Love and totally miss out on God's Agape Love. You see His Love covers all sin, yours and mine. He forgives all. God's love never fails – nor forsakes us.

Now this is for all of God's heart-bruised and persecuted ones. Are you reading this writing and feeling that the tender petals of your heart were trampled underfoot or crushed early by the insensitive thorns of life? If so, please forgive the hurt from those who hurt you. Forgive those who betrayed you. Forgive them because you've been forgiven. Most of all you

must forgive yourselves. Stop thinking you asked for or caused whatever happened to you to happen. God says in His Word in Matthew 6:33, "give and it shall be given unto you, good measure, pressed down and shaken together and running over shall men give unto your bosom this day". So GIVE for*giv*eness. Jesus loves each of us – even those caught up in error – and he suffered to show us ALL just how much he loves each of us (Galatians 5:6 "For faith... works by love).

Let me take a look at this abuse epidemic from the world's view for a moment. I've heard it asked, "Why don't people in situations like this just leave or put that abusive person out of their home? Why?"

Before the 1980s and even in some homes today, to speak of the abuses would be to bring a covering of "shame" to that home or that family's name. This was back in the day when a person's name meant or stood for something in their community. Unfortunately, protecting a good name often meant NOT protecting the helpless children or women in those families. A lot of women have been literally trapped in situations where they feel they have no hope of escaping the abuse. Like my mom, some of these women were illiterate, medically dependent, or had low self-esteem. These women were in turn abused physically, mentally and emotionally by the perpetrators who then went on to abuse the children in those homes too.

This is also the environment where a lot of children develop early tendencies towards homosexuality. Others are born with tendencies towards one sex but they are equipped with the organs of another sex; this group is called intersex or transgenders. In some cases children who are abused tend to become sexually promiscuous or even frigid in their adult relationships Some even resort to drug use and prostitution in an effort to escape from their past. But what they're really doing is going deeper and deeper into a cycle of sin. Making the path of sin's tracks clear and deadly to those looking from afar, with one sin leading to another... to another... to another and finally to hopeless despair for so many people who get caught up in this cycle of abuse. This is a cycle we can all stop from being repeated when we acknowledge what has happened to us and then when we ask for help. The best help we can ever receive is from Jesus Christ, our Perfect Healer.

So as you read this book, I pray God will begin a regeneration process in your life to renew your body, soul and spirit from the inside out. If you've suffered this kind of abuse at the hands of a friend, a family member or an enemy to the point where you felt you were drowning under a flood of violent pain and shame, yet you lived in spite of it all – **celebrate your life with joy!** Practice praising God with a loud voice! Even if you never open up your mouth and tell what happened to you to another living soul – be encouraged and lift up your head. Know that God knows what you have survived and continue to survive. Know that He *has* always provided a way of escape for you even out of your darkest nights and bleakest days. So please, receive my prayer that God is even now bringing peace and healing of the mind and body – both yours and mine. Just surrender to His Spirit and learn how to just let go. When you decide to TRUST God, you'll be able to rise up out of the ashes from your past to become an Overcomer and Victor – no longer a victim of the situation. Make an exchange (see scripture reference below) His beauty for your ashes. I guarantee you, His seed (God's Word) will meet your every need.

Isaiah 61:3

3To grant [consolation and joy] to those who mourn in Zion--to give them an ornament (a garland or diadem)

*of beauty instead of ashes, the oil of joy instead of
mourning, the garment [expressive] of praise instead
of a heavy, burdened, and failing spirit--that they
may be called oaks of righteousness [lofty, strong, and
magnificent, distinguished for uprightness, justice,
and right standing with God], the planting of the
Lord, that He may be glorified.*

*(Amplified Version can be found at
www.biblegateway.com)*

If, on the other hand, you have never been through a "night
visit" let me set one up for you: It's in the middle of the night
and there's the cover of darkness for those who are wont to
"tip and dip".... In a back bedroom, a little girl or young boy's
private parts are meticulously uncovered – not in concern,
but in violation. Whispered commands come near small ears
as big and determined hands undo clothing, hands that rub
roughly and feel clammy as they touch upon the skin of an
innocent child's body. It's an unforgettable memory of a sick
man's groping hands and lustful whispers of "'C'mon now, turn
over" . . . followed by his "shhhh, this won't hurt – jus' let me
touch it."

Sick yes, because no honorable man should ever desire
to have sexual relations with a child, especially one under his
care. Is there a penetration? No, not physically, but mentally
and emotionally – yes, the violation is complete. For me, these
"night visits" took place over a period of about six years. For
you that time may have been shorter... or longer.

Now if you've ever been into one of these dark rooms
like the one where I just took you, I'm sure you clearly get
the picture. And if you haven't, some pictures are better off
destroyed before they develop into memories that are hard for

young minds to erase. Memories not fully developed will only die when they are fully exposed to the light of God's Word. So I admonish you to hear God as he speaks to your heart. He is declaring its time for the burial. He'll tell you, "It's time to surrender your life to Jesus Christ. "When you do this all the dead things in your life will be crucified . . . and you'll be free from them to rise up out of the dirt and be at one with the Anointed One as His Anointing comes to rest upon you. It's time to fulfill your purpose and the call of God by embracing His liberty."

✐ 4*Island of Patmos*
(12/26/98 - 7:48pm @ Devin's)

Child of God - what island are you isolated upon?
Why have you allowed Satan to trap you all alone?
God's offer of life is free – open up your eyes – can't you see?
O Sinner man - O sinner woman
Do you not know that God's moat of
protection flows all around you?
Keeping you safe from the enemy . . .
Child of God - what shelters you from Satan's snare?
Where do you hide from worldly cares?
Seek ye first the Kingdom of God and His Righteousness . . .
And His Word shall be the drawbridge of
escape from your island of Patmos.

But there are ways that little girls (and boys) escape memories too full of pain and too shameful to face. They find

---

4.)   *History: My Story - His Glory (vol1)®. Copyright © 2003 Phasia* a safe place to hide. Oft-times that place will lie somewhere deep inside of the one being victimized.

I had a hiding place too. I found a way to soar far away from reality on the wings of my imagination. Television? No, it was a novelty for most families, when I was a child, the world of electronic video games and computers hadn't even been discovered yet for the typical household. No, I would escape often to my secret place through the pages of books. I read to escape . . . I escaped to read. I became a bookworm burrowing away from all the ills of my life. I read everything. I devoured books on traveling, poetry, biographies and autobiographies, westerns; even dictionaries and encyclopedias. I read books of suspense and drama, Mother Goose fairy tales, historical romance novels, science handbooks – and yes, 'adult' magazines too. I found a sense of security and protection as I hid away in my newly discovered refuge. No one could touch me there. It was a place filled with dusty corridors and even dustier books – the libraries of my youth. Whenever I was afraid, I escaped for a season – a season that lasted for years. Until I realized it wasn't me escaping, it was my mind. Whenever I finished reading whatever I was reading, the problems were still there, waiting to be faced. And my body was still there being used and abused – for weeks that led to months and months that led to years.

I was a child who quickly grew up, yet I still remained a child in so many ways. For years, I walked through life carrying a set of unruly twins in the womb of my mind. I would entertain the maturing sinful nature of one at the same time I was trying to cultivate the naïve innocent nature of the other. My baby girl dream of castles, princes and happily-ever-afters, became as unrealistic as the fairy tales they were built upon and flimsy as the paper the words were typed on. Early in life, I believe I caught a glimpse of my God-given vision, but

I kept finding myself trying to build it on the wispy clouds of an ethereal mirage that was based upon fiction and fairy tales. There was no solid foundation until much later. That's when I finally found myself in Jesus Christ and established my faith in Him – by accepting His Word, His love and His sacrifice for me.

You may be asking yourself, "Where was her mother during this time?" I must say at first, I thought my mother knew. And I thought her way of dealing with the knowledge was by escaping into her pain-free world of prescription drugs. I have vague memories of her in and out of hospitals after she attempted to overdose on pills several times. A few years ago, I got an opportunity to talk with her about it, and I remember my surprise at discovering she hadn't known. I also remember her pain. As we talked, she revealed she felt she'd failed us and had not been a good mom after she did find out what had happened. It was a revelation that I believe brought us closer together during her final years of life. I assured her that she had not failed us as a mother. She'd done the best she knew how to do based upon what she had to work with. I told her I did not blame her. She too had been a victim. Mom died one week following my 38th birthday. She was 53. God knows, I miss her so very much.

So where was my natural father in all of this? He came in and out of my life briefly until I was 13 or so. When I turned 13, he took me away to Ohio for a wonderful two weeks to live with him during the Christmas holidays up North. He even built up enough nerves to ask me about the rumors of abuse. I didn't confide in him. I didn't really know or trust him then. Besides by then the "night visits" had come to an end. He hadn't been there before to show he cared when they were happening, so I never thought he really wanted to know. He didn't pursue the matter. In the summer of 2004 Dad was killed in a hit and run incident. He had mentioned what he thought had happened and how he didn't know how to deal with the rumors of abuse the summer before his death when we discussed the incident by phone. I remember that Dad's voice clearly communicated his anger. That alone let me know that he had cared. I have forgiven him too. As for God, well I didn't know enough about Him at the time to know He cared more deeply than any one and was deeply saddened by my abuse. But I do believe that my reading wasn't just an escape, it was also a coping mechanism. I was afraid and whenever I couldn't cope, I would escape into the pages of someone else's life.

Yes, I heard your unasked question earlier, "So you escaped to things like playboy huh?" In my ignorance, I fed the hunger being awakened in my body by reading material that supported those feelings. Yet I read the Bible too. Though I barely understood what I read at the time nor could I pronounce half of the words I read as a child., I clearly remember my struggle to read what the old folks called "The Good Book" all the way through. Though I must admit the Bible stories were more interesting at that age than the actual scriptures. The book of Revelation still brings to mind the marvelous wonders I discovered of a promised future.

However, my favorite scriptures were found in the *Book of Psalm – the 23rd, the 27th, and the 100th Psalm*. They were the nighttime soldiers who stayed at their posts and kept me safe. They watched over me and guarded me from the storms of evil and bondage that came like battering rams to attack my young mind daily – and my young body every night. They promised real freedom – and they promised real protection. I anchored myself with all the yearning hope of a young child outside a glass-front candy store into those promises.

Those promises didn't fail me. A break finally came for me from the constant abuse. They didn't stop totally at first but the episodes became less frequent. It was after we moved from the "city projects" back into the country where Mom's Daddy lived. Granddaddy, or Daddy as we called him, soon became the only man I felt I could totally trust. You see Daddy wasn't that tall in stature – in fact he was barely 5 feet 4 inches – but his power was clearly felt, and in my eyes he stood feet taller than any giants of fear in my mind ever did. A dark-complexioned man, Daddy looked as though he could have been sculpted out of the rich, fertile and the hard-packed soil he owned and lovingly farmed. It was a farm he ruled with an iron hand, and whoever was on his property did what he told them to do – or they weren't on it for very long. To back it up, he had several guns he didn't hesitate to use if pushed. I felt protected and loved in his presence. I felt necessary and useful. I felt secure and sheltered. It was a new experience and my first introduction to someone who lived in their God-given purpose.

In looking at Daddy, I learned about God in the flesh before I ever read about Him in a book. First, like God, Daddy was a property man, just on a smaller scale. He owned 38 acres of family land complete with cattle and crops. That was like a little kingdom to a child of 10 or eleven. Even now, I can clearly smell the rank, yet fertile scents of farm life. Goats had a wild scent and taste that was captured in the toughness of their meat. I recall the sour ripe smell of the hogs as they wallowed in their mud ponds. When I used to taste the saltiness of bacon or pan-fried sausage – I remembered. I still remember how it felt to slaughter an animal – their warm blood as it clung to the hands that stuck the knife in their throats with a killing blow. It was their death for our life – they were the food given for our survival. Those experiences were both frightening and exciting. Jesus is the same for us today. His life-giving blood streamed warmly down at His death to soak into the greedy earth. His life was given for our lives as told in 2 Corinthians 5:21 (King James Version).

> *For he hath made him to be **sin** for us, **who
> knew no sin**; that we might be made the
> righteousness of God in him.*

I remember "chunking" watermelons onto trucks and tractor-trailers. I remember the aching backs and sore arms. I remember those cold rides behind a tractor on the tobacco planter as we took turns sticking shoots of tobacco plants in that wet, sucking, gritty black dirt. I remember the cold ears and colder noses. I remember the backbreaking work of picking peas, okra and sweet potatoes; and "shucking" itchy ears of corn from miles of green and yellow corn stalks. I remember pretending that fresh ears of corn with its silky golden hair were dolls. I remember the sunshine. I remember the smell of boiled peanuts being bagged for the Labor Day festivals. I remember me and my older sister making and baking "mud-pies" in one of Grandma's old ovens that sat outside in their backyard. I remember playing "church" as we mimicked people and the funny things we'd see take place in our Baptist church services – something I believe every young child at one time or another did while growing up. I remember the smiles and the love. I remember running from my brother into the front gate to Daddy's yard and chipping my front tooth. It's not chipped today. God has restored it just as He has restored my 50-year-old body back to a state of youthfulness.

I remember thinking that a funeral meant you hung a person's body up on a skeleton rack and people came to say good-bye because they were sad that that person was gone. I remember singing in the choir and loving to go to church. I remember my sister and I singing with ears of corn as our microphones. Our stage was the back of a tractor trailer bed. I remember the "peach-tree switches" Daddy would use when we'd disobeyed him. I remember his infamous "Betsy", a strap of rubber cut from a tire that was never far from Daddy's hand. It was truly his rod of correction he'd threaten us with when we disobeyed his orders – and it was something he only had to use ONCE on my siblings and me. I remember learning how to drive – and almost running Daddy over with his tractor the first time he let me try steering on my own.

Through all this, I remember the "smell and taste of life" there on the farm – it was the smell and taste of summer that always brings a smile and causes my eyes to well up with tears. These memories all remind me I had hope and I still managed to be a happy, strong and carefree child, rejoicing in my youth. Best of all I remember always having food and clothes and love and – and protection. It wasn't always said out loud but it was felt. Daddy's very presence signified and guaranteed it. These fruits are being replanted into my new memory book. So the seeds can take root and be replanted in my children and my future prosperity . . . for a better legacy.

Yes, he was my hero because he was also an honorable man. If Daddy gave you his word, it was better than a written contract. We knew it as his family, and his partners and the business folks he dealt with knew it. He was a man with a heart like God. He didn't lie. If he didn't agree with you, he just told you so. He loved to talk, but he was not garrulous – unless he was drunk. And though he loved a good beer or glass of his own homemade "moonshine" every weekend, he was not a mean drunk. I saw Daddy laugh and play with us more than at any other time when he took a "sip" of his home grown brew. To me, Daddy was his word. I pray and hope he's now resting with God . . . as they wait on us all to finish what we were sent to do here and so we can all go home to be with the Lord.

Living on my grandfather's farm, I remember Grandma reading her Bible each night. Afterwards she and I would climb down out of her warm high bed, kneel on the cold wooden floor and pray before we climbed back into its comforting warmth to go to sleep. She was my very first teacher of the Word of God. I followed her teachings all the way through college. Sometimes I remember falling asleep right there on my knees as I talked with God. I didn't know much about listening to Him then. I didn't know the communication was supposed to be two-way — even though that was my major. I didn't get the revelation until much later. Now I know we are supposed to develop and have a relationship with God, and not just humans. That's why He calls it fellowship or a close association of friendship or comradeship. But I do know that those times would always give me hope and refresh me. I would feel the Word working around me to chase away all the "boogie men." Now I cry inside because sometimes Grandma who at the writing of this book seems to be lost in the "august season" of her winter years — with a dim memory of her faith and hope in God. But maybe she just sees a clearer vision that gives her more peace because it has drawn her closer to Him over the years. I pray she is with our LORD and JESUS now, worshipping and praising HIS beauty.

Yes our grandparents' farm became the safe farm-like Garden of Eden where I began to excel and prosper. I began to dream of traveling the world to places like Spain and France, Germany and Scotland, Ireland and England. I wanted to travel the states too, but not as much as I wanted to travel overseas. I developed pen pals in France and Greece — Bruno was from France and there was a girl from Greece. Her name escapes me now, but we corresponded for a few years and even exchanged our pictures. In junior high I took Spanish and French classes and by the standards of my foreign language teacher, I was better than most students were. And through it all – one thing remained constant – I continued to read. I would stay up all night reading in my closet after everyone else thought I'd gone to sleep. Then I'd jump in the bed minutes before it was time to get up for school. I read on the bus. I read in class. I read in church. I read everywhere as my energy and my desire to know more about life grew. On the other hand, I began to dream more of being somebody special and important in this world. These dreams chased after me even at night after I closed my eyes in sleep. They came also in the form of memorable visions that I recall even today. They were biblical visions I believe were formed by things I'd read out of the book of the Revelation.

A stigmatized 'project' child turned country girl; I enjoyed my grandfather's farm. In fact, I loved it. It's where I made 'the stand'. I remember the incident clearly, but not so much the details that lead up to it. As usual, it was late at night. We were older, maybe late elementary or early junior high students. The "night visits" were still taking place and he was becoming bolder. Now I must digress to say until I started writing this book, my sister and I have never, ever discussed these "night visits" between us, not any of it. We were both victims, but whereas I escaped into my companion of books – I'm not sure how she escaped (or if she ever really did). Sometimes I want to ask her, but . . .. Maybe, I'm afraid of the answer I'll receive. I hope she will read this book too.

So the night visits had gotten bolder and more frequent, partially I believe, because our bodies were becoming more developed and starting to mature. We were young girls in the beginning stages of puberty, wanting to "experiment" more with boys. And what's tastier than what you've already been nibbling on – and yet is still proving to be out of reach? I

23

believe this made us more desirable as the "forbidden" fruit to our mother's boyfriend.

The night I recall, Mom and her live in lover were having another fight. Those had become more frequent too. But as time went on she'd become sicker and was not able to fend off his fists or harsh words as easily as she once had. She was physically her own personal jailer with the help of her prescription pills, which she used to try and escape from narcoleptic seizures. She was emotionally drained by the disappointments of her life and defeated after giving her heart unwisely to another who was out of her reach. This last, my sisters and I learned after her death.

[5]**Narcolepsy** - *A disorder characterized by sudden and uncontrollable, though often-brief attacks of deep sleep, sometimes accompanied by paralysis and hallucinations.*

So she couldn't handle it and was giving up bit by bit but her abusive boyfriend wasn't helping the matter. Interestingly enough, I believe he did actually love her in his own way. She always would say she believed he'd put what the old country folks called "roots" – a form of dark island-like religious witchcraft – on her. She would say, "He has messed me up for any other man." And even when she was declaring she hated him, she'd let him back into her home. I believe "roots" is something you can choose to let have power over you if you put your belief in it, just as you can choose to let sin reign in your heart. <u>Any</u> belief or action gains power once you put faith to work on its behalf.

[5.] *The American Heritage® Dictionary of the English Language, Fourth Edition. Copyright © 2000 by Houghton Mifflin Company. Published by Houghton Mifflin Company. All rights reserved.*

Well this time he'd gone too far, I'd had enough. I felt something snap inside of me. I don't remember how I got it from the kitchen, but suddenly I stood barefoot just inside Mom's room in my little white nightgown. I was holding one of her 13" butcher knives in my hand and calmly telling her abusive boyfriend that if he did not get out of her house right now 'I would kill him.' He looked at me and knew I meant it. I didn't yell or scream it out in hysterics. I didn't tremble. I stood there and quietly told him what would happen if he ever touched her again with his fists. I felt the power I held and he believed me. He backed away that night – all the time calling me crazy and telling my mom I was crazy – but he left. He didn't come back for several days. What is interesting is that by me taking a stand against him abusing my mom, I took a stand also against the abuse I was suffering at his hand.

The night visits completely stopped. Since that time he's always been cautious and watchful around me. And to my knowledge he never ever hit my mom again.

Unfortunately, by then my flesh had been trained and initiated into the world of sexual sin. This time it was by my own hand that the abuse continued as my body hungered and craved to be touched. I remember for years later, even into my marriage, I would masturbate to get the same breathless and forbidden feelings of arousal that I'd experienced from those night visits. Then I'd feel greatly ashamed for the self-inflicted act that I would commit only in solitude. I was ashamed of the feelings I purposely stirred up. I also remember not feeling anything with the actual sex act – not unless I stirred up my mind to feel something. For me, all the feelings and excitement seemed to evolve around the prelude or foreplay of the actual sex act. It was all about the *arousal and the stimulation* before the act. Unnaturally for a female, I tended to get more excited from engaging in sex-related visuals and thoughts – probably like most men would get from looking at pictures or watching dirty movies. Everything else was a letdown. I believe that was one of the scars the night rituals left behind.

Did my step-dad rape me – not physically, but mentally and emotionally I'm not so sure anymore. No, the *physical rape* actually came later. It happened when I was 15. Was it because I began reading *too much too soon*? Was it because of what I'd already "experienced" in sexual matters? I still ask myself those questions today. Only God knows, He knows I'm not a psychoanalyst.

In my jaded, yet girlish eyes the one who finally took my virginity was made up of the stuff written about in romance novels. He had the clean-cut chiseled features of a classic Ebony Fashion Fair model. That along with thick and wavy black hair framing a pair of piercing black eyes and soft-looking lips you read about in romantic novels and that seemed as if they were designed especially for kisses. All this was wrapped up in a chocolatey-brown 5-foot-7 frame that knew the ins and outs of basketball courts and baseball fields and had lounged in its share of pool halls. When he spoke in his low-pitched voice with just the right amount of sexy huskiness – it was a voice that instantly brought to my young mind the vision of dampened hot sheets with sweaty-bodies entangled upon them. He was charismatic, confident and composed. He embodied all my youthful fantasies of a perfect man, in body if not in spirit. He was my cousin, albeit a distant one.

I had always shared sexy banter and joked around with him. He knew I had a crush on him in fact my sister dated his cousin. We all thought they'd end up getting married – Jules and Steve, but I think he cheated on her and she wasn't very forgiving. Their relationship ended from that incident. Anyway, this distant cousin invited me to go with him for a short drive one night – the actual time and date fails me now, but I do remember it was a mid-summer night. I had on a pair of short shorts or as they were called back then, "hot pants." My sister and her beau had disappeared somewhere in the dark to court each other and so they were not really keeping a close eye on me – or on him.

So we took off and drove further back in the woods, like we were going back to my home from the back way. Only he stopped midway, in the thick of the woods – in the dark of the night. I felt grown up and complimented by his interest. I should have felt wary. I believe we talked – briefly. We kissed a lot. Things got heavy, including the petting, and I remember asking him to stop, but I didn't stop letting him kiss me or push him away, so he didn't stop. I said "don't" like I'd read heroines in those romance books I'd been reading say it – with no power and in a way that I now know actually meant don't stop and he didn't... stop. I'd flirted too close and too long with danger and things got too hot. It hurt. He hurt me. We hurt our families . . . we hurt each other. For my role in all that took place between us that night, I find that it's now my turn to say I'm sorry. I must publicly apologize for leading him on to the point of no return.

After we finally drove back to the place we'd left from, we found that people had been searching for us because we'd been gone for so long. My sister and I left and went home. Mom knew by looking at my shorts what had happened. We went to the local hospital emergency room. I'll never forget that night. Doctors ran tests and I was given some medicine. Police reports were filed. Officials and family members asked questions and listened to answers. The blame game got started. All the time, I felt guilty. I felt at fault. I felt I had led him on. I felt I deserved what had happened. It was a classic victim's syndrome . . . left feeling that maybe I hadn't been a victim. Maybe he was the victim. Cycles of abuse can be vicious and spread further than we believe possible when we don't get the healing our minds and bodies need from God's Word.

The other thing I remember about the hospital that night. One of the two medicines they'd given me caused a reaction, a bad one. My tongue tried to double-back down into my throat. They had to use tongue depressors to it from trying to go down my throat and choking me to death. Afterwards, they said I was allergic to medication containing zinc. (Twenty years later I discovered zinc is what helps build and keep the immune system healthy. I believe this was Satan's early attempt in my life to try destroying me from the inside out – but I keep reminding him that he won't prosper. He didn't prosper then, and he won't prosper now. I have repented of those sins. I have wisdom superabundantly guiding me in the ways I should go. I trust God with my whole heart.)

The following weeks were a blur. During that first week, one of our church mothers saved me from being hit and run over. I had apparently walked in front of her car as she drove down the highway near my home. I was so dazed by the medicine I was given to take after the rape that I didn't see or hear her car as I walked back home from visiting my cousin Sabrina's house. It was a time of trials and disappointments for our family. We stood protectively together in the face of hurtful and hate-filled comments – as people showed they were only people who were hurting or wanted to hurt others.

My sister and her boyfriend almost didn't weather the aftermath of that storm. But the familial strain along with an indiscretion finally cracked their relationship apart and caused it to bitterly end years later. For the most part, people forgot and some even forgave. But I'd learned my lesson the hard way. Real life does not always end like fairy tales with 'happily-ever-after.'

We hand weapons over to the enemy to use against us when

we allow weaknesses to become strongholds from our past. Our weaknesses allow Satan to gain *toeholds* into our lives each time we are encouraged to compromise. He and his demons use things and circumstances of pressure to try to get us to stop believing in "God" for the small things His Word promises to manifest into our lives. Then if we allow that, the enemy plants a *foothold* by trying to direct us away from the Plan and Purpose God has for us. Each step by the enemy that we allow in our lives turns into a *stronghold* that becomes *generational curses* as the enemy develops his power over us.

⁶*Strongholds*
(03/19/02 – 11:29am)

~Breaking the chains that bind your mind
Breaking the cords that control your life
Freeing your spirit to rule your soul
What are the strongholds keeping you from what's right?
Are they generational curses from your mother?
Are they hereditary curses from your father?
Are you able to see them in the history of your family?
Then, yes, you too can break free.
~You see – Jesus Christ already paid the going rate
To set you free and not a moment too late
He has already petitioned the Father on behalf of your case
Saying, "Daddy, my blood was the recompense"
~So you are no longer the weakest link
Because that old stronghold is now a broken fence
Satan the strong man, has been defeated
by THE MAN Jesus Christ

6.) *History: My Story - His Glory (vol1)®. Copyright © 2003 Phasia*

And He has taken residence once and for all in your life
~When you stood in your liberty in Jesus Christ
The Anointed One and His Anointing set you free
There are no more "sacred" closets or hiding places
Satan and his demons have had to flee
~Your life is open now and free to all scrutiny
In faith you are declared more than a conqueror
Your righteousness in Christ Jesus is your key
As you stand forever in unity with the Holy Trinity

I've always felt, even to this day that it was my fault. You see I flirted a lot. I enjoyed practicing the skills that I'd only read about in books. I wanted to see if they really worked or not. So I developed a huge crush on a number of older men. First was this guy a couple years out of high school when I was in 7th grade. But our interaction only consisted of one or two kisses, club dancing and some long phone chats. I guess looking back; I was what some would have called cute or pretty. Like now, I had long, beautifully thick hair. I was thin, but I had slight curves that made me look female and I was always well dressed. All except for my teeth – which I felt needed braces. You see they protrude because of an overbite. But I made up for that by always having a smile on my face.

⁷*Appearances*
(12/27/98 - 11:30pm @ Lena's)

Who are we, and are we who we appear to be?
Why do we pretend?
Do we seek to impress friends?

Friends would never need a façade
They take you as you are made
With true friends, you can be real
And show how you truly feel
There is no need to hide
They know what you feel inside
So why do we put on appearances?
Don't we know they can never truly cover
the pain hidden within us?
They are like foundational powders
They wash off with our tears
And they never, ever allow us to be real

I had several names outside of my given name as I was growing up. Red-bones – for my complexion; stringbeans – for my long legs and slender size (plus it was a name I shared with my older sister); bookworm – because of my consuming hobby and love of reading; Farrah Fawcett – for my long hair, usually worn flipped; and 'horsey' – for my two front buckteeth. I considered those last two nicknames detestable, knowing those who used them were not saying them to compliment me.

Like most girls with a physical complex or self-esteem problem, I thrived off of compliments. I was always an A/B honor student, but in the last couple years of high school I got caught up in what normally draws most teens away from the books and pursuit of learning – the aphrodisiac of "party time" and boys.

So why am I telling you all of this? I admit it's been therapeutic for me. But it's a healing process I pray you can partake of too. If you wonder why I called this book "homegrown"? It's because I've grown, hopefully closer to the home of God's Kingdom from the teachings of the many very enlightened teachers and Pastors who have been my inspiration.

One of these teachers has been Bishop T.D. Jakes, who recently wrote a booked called "Naked, and Not Ashamed." *In it he says that we all have been given seeds of uniqueness . . . seeds of greatness from God. But we must not be ashamed by what caused those seeds to form and in some cases those seeds need to be revealed. Bishop says we need to nurture them and to allow God to use them.* (And I paraphrase him). I needed to hear that, and I believe that someone needs to hear my story too.

Some of the great teachers in my life have been my spiritual parents: Bishop George L. and Pastor April R. Davis; along with Joyce Meyer, Dr. Myles Monroe, Kenneth and Gloria Copeland, Dr. Creflo Dollar, and many other great men and women of God. There are other Impact Church ministry Pastors and teachers who have been constantly feeding the Word into my life and holding me accountable to God to walk in being God's *best me I can be* according to all that I'm being taught. For that, I am truly thankful.

It's called "HomeGrown", because that's what each of us are when we pull away all of the camouflage – the weeds. Like the unforgettable burning taste of hot moonshine and or that cooling draught of "country iced water" – the wild bittersweet juiciness of blackberries, and the sweet tartness of homegrown peaches, both canned in an old-fashioned Mason jar, it's who I am. I'm a country girl who's been 'HomeGrown' from seeds of Love that were planted inside of me and sealed above by my heavenly Father. Like harvest cultivated fruit that you can't pick up just anywhere, because they're grown for a special purpose, so am I. They were HIS seeds that were planted inside of me before thoughts of me were even conceived in the mind of my parents. HIS purpose for me existed before I did.

HIS seeds of purpose exist despite the weeds of self-abuse and childhood molestation. Those seeds were resistant to those same weeds because our Heavenly Father knew beforehand what was needed in the seed to make those shoots strong enough to survive. And now I know He's counting on me to allow Him to nurture and prune them into the trees of prosperity and purpose for others to feed and feast upon. To manifest finally into the forest of faith He's anointed and called me to be. I know God wants me to be a witness of His grace and goodness for the entire world to see. I am HIS forest of love, offering forgiveness and hope, and giving emotional and physical release to millions of men and women who have been hiding behind their pride – and their pain.

Men and women who were like me, hiding their shame from behind the inadequate fig tree leaves of deception planted by the enemy. The saddest part is when we try hiding from God in our garden of disobedience and despair. I've been there to that garden a few times. The only thing I found there were the rotten seeds from the fruits of disobedience birthed so long ago by our parents Adam and Eve in their Garden of Eden. *The story of their disobedience and deception is recorded in Genesis 3:7, 8 (New King James Version) as is the story of others who were blinded like them in 2 Timothy 3 (The Message).* **They were all self-deceived and walking in darkness.** This is why the Bible is so clear in its warning to us to be continually alert to the tricks of the enemy, even to our inward enemies of self-denial and selfishness.

> *¹Don't be naive. There are difficult times ahead. ²As the end approaches, people are going to be self-absorbed, money-hungry, self-promoting, stuck-up, profane, contemptuous of parents, crude, coarse,*

³*dog-eat-dog, unbending, slanderers,*
impulsively wild, savage, cynical,
⁴*treacherous, ruthless, bloated windbags,*
addicted to lust, and allergic to God.
⁵*They'll make a show of religion, but behind*
the scenes they're animals. Stay clear of
these people.
⁶*These are the kind of people who smooth-*
talk themselves into the homes of unstable
and needy women and take advantage
of them; women who, depressed by their
sinfulness, take up with every new religious
fad that calls itself "truth." ⁷*They get*
exploited every time and never really learn.
⁸*These men are like those old Egyptian*
frauds Jannes and Jambres, who challenged
Moses. They were rejects from the faith,
twisted in their thinking, defying truth
itself. ⁹*But nothing will come of these latest*
impostors. Everyone will see through them,
just as people saw through that Egyptian
hoax.

Keep the Message Alive

¹⁰*You've been a good apprentice to me, a*
part of my teaching, my manner of life,
direction, faith, steadiness, love, patience,
¹¹*troubles, sufferings--suffering along with*
me in all the grief I had to put up with in
Antioch, Iconium, and Lystra. And you also
well know that God rescued me! ¹²*Anyone*
who wants to live all out for Christ is in for

a lot of trouble; there's no getting around
it. [13]*Unscrupulous con men will continue to*
exploit the faith. They're as deceived as the
people they lead astray. As long as they are
out there, things can only get worse.
[14]*But don't let it faze you. Stick with what*
you learned and believed, sure of the
integrity of your teachers-- [15]*why, you took*
in the sacred Scriptures with your mother's
milk! There's nothing like the written Word
of God for showing you the way to salvation
through faith in Christ Jesus. [16]*Every part*
of Scripture is God-breathed and useful one
way or another--showing us truth, exposing
our rebellion, correcting our mistakes,
training us to live God's way. [17]*Through the*
Word we are put together and shaped up for
the tasks God has for us.
(The Message Bible version see www.
biblegateway.com)

I cannot boast of anything good that I've done – outside of accepting Jesus Christ as my Savior and my Lord. In fact I'm actually ashamed to admit to some of things I've done. So why do I peel layer upon layer off of my life for others to turn up their noses at or avert their eyes from me in possible condemnation? Why not just leave it all unsaid you may even be thinking? Because I was given this assignment, "my survival *from me* depends upon it coming to the Light to help deliver others."

The Light will root out the darkness from my mind, grain by grain. It won't be able to find shelter to continue growing its filth in my heart or allow sin to develop any of its deadly rag weeds over my mind. I am allowing my mind to be renewed by the Word and my life to be transformed by God's Spirit. So are you hiding something you feel no one else would ever understand or accept about you? Then come to the Truth of God's Word and receive His Holy Spirit. They are both here for the asking and ready to purify and nurture you back into His presence if you're lost. Are you ready? I hope so, because it promises to be a shake it up, country bumpy, revealing ride for many (especially for me). I just pray that it's the right time to say and reveal what shall be said and revealed in this book. If it's not, I pray for God to release that timing to me so I won't be too late sharing it and the pruning process that's been necessary in my life with you. I'm desiring to be in His will and constantly walking in His favor. It's my prayer for you too, in Jesus' Name. Amen!

✐ *⁸Sanctuary*

(1/4/03 – 9:01pm, rev. 11/1/03 – 3:28pm)

Dear God make me a Sanctuary
For all the masses
A place they come for healing
From all their messes
Lord Jesus you've made me
Into a Sanctuary
For all God's people
Holy Spirit thank you for being
A Sanctuary for me

8.) *History: The Poetic Tapestry of My Life (vol2)®. Copyright ©*
2003 Phasia

Homegrown Seed . . .

Great pressure does one of two things – it brings out the beauty within or it crushes. This writing came out during a time in my life when I was experiencing great pressure in many different areas of my life. I was living a life that felt unreal. I say unreal because I would do and say exactly opposite of the way I would feel. And I did this because I was being taught not to be dependent upon my feelings or my emotions, because they were very unreliable and always changing – so unlike God's Word. So day by day I would fight **me** and things that tempted **me** to stay <u>outside of</u> God's will. I knew there was a purpose, and I felt that this book was one of those purposes God has designed my life to produce. There were internal battles raging inside: The battle to do "good"; against the battle to be totally selfish and destructive. What really was strange was I knew even at the time of being placed in the heat of the battle that certain thoughts and actions were totally outside of God's will. I was given a choice. We are all given choices according to God's Word in Deuteronomy 30:19 (King James Version).

*This day I call heaven and earth as witnesses against you that I have set before you **life** and death, blessings and curses. Now **choose life**, so that you and your children may live.*

Every day I had to keep reminding myself that I am strong and strengthened by God's word. His anointing is upon me. I kept telling myself that God would be disappointed in my thoughts – but God would tell me at those times – Phasia I made you. I knew what your thoughts would be even before you did. I knew before you chose what choices you would make, but I still upheld you. I didn't want you to make the wrong choices, but I allowed you to operate in your God-given right of a free will. Still some thoughts God was disappointed in whenever I would allow myself to go that step further and act on those thoughts. Choices can actually become no choice at all when you're trying to walk the straight and narrow way.

This is what I've heard God say to me when I've felt or gotten too close to the edge . . . *"You're trying to hide your feelings and emotions because you haven't yet learned how to be honest about them. You allow shame from your past to trap you into feeling what you feel. You don't see the full picture of your life like I do, but you're getting there. Each day my Word grows deeper and deeper in your heart as its roots in your spirit grow stronger and more secure in Me. Your stony ground is becoming "good ground" according to my Word in Mark 4. You don't have all the answers in your head but you're coming to realize that I do have all the answers and because my Spirit LIVES on the inside of you – you do know what to do."*

So I encourage you as I've been told by many "do not be discouraged". I'm telling you don't quit or give up. Instead recognize and know that your life is in God's hand. I didn't give up. I will make it and so will you if you stay the course. Don't give up. God has said, you may not be able to please others but He didn't put you here to please others. Your purpose in this world is to become a godly seed and to please God.

✐ ⁹*Purpose To Be Me*
(10/15/03 – 7:07pm)

__I am completed__ in love by God's design
Uniquely made, I'm one of a kind
I'm called for a purpose to be me
__I am naked__ and exposed before the eyes of God
Like the Apostle Peter my life is his fishing rod
I'm gifted in my purpose to be me
__I am refined__ by this life into a master key
Destined for an expected end in God's eternity
I'm created for God's purpose to be me

9

Homegrown Tree . . .

"From the fruit of his words a man shall be
satisfied with good, and the work of a man's hands
shall come back to him [as a harvest]."
~ Proverbs 12:14 Amplified ~

A lot of us could nearly be "saints" but our actions towards those we interact with in the world. Most of us gripe and complain about our life's situations. We carry around baggage from the past, gladly suffering in our trials, because we think its what makes us better Christians or just plain better people. But Jesus has already suffered for us. He's already paid all the costs for our pains and our hang-ups. So why do we feel we need to feel bad? A lot of us divide what we do, think or say up into categories of good or bad. But it's not really about that. What it is all about is the fruit of your tree. What are you producing for others to see? No, I'm not saying you can't make mistakes or other people can't make mistakes, but what I am saying is don't have a week-long or year-long or life-long pity party. No body wants to come. We pity ourselves when we judge or criticize something done (or something we think shouldn't e done) to us by others. We need to become mature trees of life and we need to stop judging and criticizing others. Do God (and yourself) a favor. It's over, so let it go. (Notice I "canned"

that phrase before Elsa did in the *Frozen* Disney movie – LOL)
Don't allow all the pain and abuse from your past to continually
cause you to keep making mistakes. Grow up!

Matthew 7:1-20

*[1]DO NOT judge and criticize and condemn others,
so that you may not be judged and criticized and
condemned yourselves.*

*[2]For just as you judge and criticize and condemn others,
you will be judged and criticized and condemned, and
in accordance with the measure you [use to] deal out
to others, it will be dealt out again to you.*

*[3]Why do you [1] stare from without at the [2] very small
particle that is in your brother's eye but do not become
aware of and consider the beam [3] of timber that is in
your own eye?*

*[4]Or how can you say to your brother, Let me get the
tiny particle out of your eye, when there is the beam [4]
of timber in your own eye?*

*[5]You hypocrite, first get the beam of timber out of your
own eye, and then you will see clearly to take the tiny
particle out of your brother's eye.*

*[6]Do not give that which is holy (the sacred thing) to
the dogs, and do not throw your pearls before hogs, lest
they trample upon them with their feet and turn and
tear you in pieces.*

7[5] Keep on asking and it will be given you; [6] keep on seeking and you will find; [7] keep on knocking [reverently] and [the door] will be opened to you.

8For everyone who keeps on asking receives; and he who keeps on seeking finds; and to him who keeps on knocking, [the door] will be opened.

9Or what man is there of you, if his son asks him for a loaf of bread, will hand him a stone?

10Or if he asks for a fish, will hand him a serpent?

11If you then, evil as you are, know how to give good and [8] advantageous gifts to your children, how much more will your Father Who is in heaven [perfect as He is] give good and [9] advantageous things to those who [10] keep on asking Him!

12So then, whatever you desire that others would do to and for you, even so do also to and for them, for this is (sums up) the Law and the Prophets.

13Enter through the narrow gate; for wide is the gate and spacious and broad is the way that leads away to destruction, and many are those who are entering through it.

14But the gate is narrow (contracted [11] by pressure) and the way is straitened and compressed that leads away to life, and few are those who find it. [L]

15Beware of false prophets, who come to you dressed as sheep, but inside they are devouring wolves. (2)

16You will [12] fully recognize them by their fruits. Do people pick grapes from thorns, or figs from thistles?

17Even so, every healthy (sound) tree bears good fruit [[13] worthy of admiration], but the sickly (decaying, worthless) tree bears bad (worthless) fruit.

18A good (healthy) tree cannot bear bad (worthless) fruit, nor can a bad (diseased) tree bear [14] excellent fruit [worthy of admiration].

19Every tree that does not bear good fruit is cut down and cast into the fire.

20Therefore, you will [15] fully know them by their fruits.

(Amplified version* also see www.biblegateway.com for this entire text online)

Show cross-references

1. Deut. 30:19; Jer. 21:8.
2. Ezek. 22:27.

Many of us have heard the oft-quoted phrase; "the fruit doesn't fall far from the tree." There's actually more truth than most care to admit in that phrase. I wouldn't have admitted to it before but I believe I've always been a little pompous, manipulative, and arrogant. My belief that I knew what was best for those I was involved with only produced more bad fruit in my life. This teamed up with the twin spirits of self-incrimination and judgmental condemnation, caused me to get involved in a lot of unhealthy relationships.

I lusted, literally lusted after love. Not sex, but love. Unfortunately, my memories of love were all tied to sex. I thought my stepfather loved me and that's why he molested me. I thought in his own way, my cousin loved me and that's why he raped me. I thought my boyfriends loved me and that's why they used my body for their own gratification. Don't misunderstand me, I understood the difference between physical sex and courting. But I equated approval to love, and whenever someone showed me approval or affirmed who I thought I was – I felt the only way I could express my love for them was by giving them my body. I did this most times not feeling anything deeper towards them than admiration. My search and intense desire for love caused me to do things in my life that I have since regretted and say things I didn't really need to say. I chased after love… and it proved to be an illusive catch. You could almost say I was a stalker of the emotion. At the time, I didn't understand what and who LOVE really exemplified. If I thought you had something to make me feel whole and complete, I would cling to you. That applied to both good and bad relationships. It also meant that my good relationships didn't last, because I proved to be such a "needy" person. I smothered others with my behavior and my needs.

Being a survivor of molestation, I also know how you can become co-dependent on others to approve of you. *According to the online dictionary.com, co-dependency means to be mutually dependent; or it relates to a relationship in which one person is psychologically dependent in an unhealthy way on someone who is addicted to a drug or self-destructive behavior, such as chronic gambling.*

Men I would typically get involved with were usually

already involved in a meaningful relationship with someone else. Meaning they were either married or close enough to being so that it didn't make a difference in legalities. That also meant that there was no chance of them having to establish a commitment to me. So basically, I would unconsciously set myself up for heartbreak and failure – by stepping outside of God's perfect will and continue to get caught up in these illicit relationships. It's almost like I didn't think I deserved any better from life and men. I don't know the exact reason why this was the case for me, but I do believe it goes back to my childhood and the trauma of the abuse I had suffered and internalized. Most times these "relationships" would end in pain or broken friendships, leaving me with the sense that I'd lost more than I'd ended up hoping to gain.

In 1999, I begin to receive some honest and straightforward teaching from Bishop George and Pastor April Davis, my spiritual father and mother. They counseled me and eventually my estranged husband when we were in the process of divorcing because of my adulterous behavior – thus saving our marriage with the power of God's Word. It was the first step in helping me to finally start figuring out my problem. I couldn't get it right as long as I kept doing it the wrong way. Sex with someone other than your marital partner or even sex outside of marriage as a single man or woman *is* the wrong way in the eyes of God. You gain a piece of that person into your physical and emotional memory banks that can never be erased, yet you also lose precious pieces of yourself that can never be regained.

I praise God for having been more than blessed than most in escaping the consequences of my actions from those incidents. God's mercy has clearly been upon my life, not allowing me to be stricken with any life-threatening or debilitating diseases from those wrong relationships. Yes, I am truly blessed and I praise God every time I recall His favor and mercy upon my life. I realize that not everyone is as fortunate or as blessed to have escaped the tempter's snare.

✐ ¹⁰*Touch The Hem of His Garment*
(3/23 /03 – 6:20pm)

The woman *with the issue of blood …for 12 years*
Kept saying in her heart …and through her tears
If I just touch the hem of the garment …of
the Anointed One standing near
I'll have a brand new start …if I reach
out in faith without any fear
So she pressed *on ahead and put legs to her faith*
She did not hesitate . . . she did not wait
She reached out and with the lightest of touches Jesus felt
His Power for healing released by her
faith and desire for wholeness
So a lesson to you *when seeking His Power and Grace*
Trust in the Word's promises and put
some action behind your faith

Luke 8:42-44 KJV

Homegrown Free . . .

Songwriter David Meece wrote a poem about "My Father's Chair" which he later recorded into a song. Check out the song sometime. It clearly describes the relationship we should have with our real Father – the Lord God. After hearing Meece speak on one of Dr. James Dobson's radio programs, I did an *online search and came across the following... "My Father's Chair" stands out as easily the most memorable and challenging song on Meece's current album "Once In A Lifetime." The song proceeds through images of three "Father's" chairs: Meece's own earthly father's chair that sat in a room and was always empty when young David needed love; a current chair that Meece sits in and tries his best to be a father for his children; and a chair in a heavenly throne room that is sat upon by One who loves Meece beyond compare and always is available for a believer who wants to sit in and talk to "Abba Father."

(*see http://www.etext.org/Religious.Texts/Lighthouse/lighthouse-2.6.txt for the entire article on this artist online)

I also found Meece's official WebPages, on which he was kind enough and trusting enough to place the lyrics of his entire album upon. Here's the poem and lyrics from "My Father's Chair."

47

My Father's Chair

My father's chair, sat in an empty room
My father's chair, covered with sheets of gloom
My father's chair through all the years
And all the tears I cried in vain
No one was there in my father's chair.

~

Sometimes at night I sit all alone
Drifting asleep in a chair of my own
When sweet sleepy eyes peer down from the hall

(Lyrics taken from online at David Meece's official
website: http://www.davidmeece.com/once2.html)

Home Grown . . .

Like most everybody else, I admit I love knowing a good secret – but in my lifetime I've learned that keeping some secrets will make your soul rot. While sharing others will keep you alive, and possibly give life to someone else who's headed down the wrong path of life.

Which indeed is the least of all seeds: but
when it is grown, it is the greatest among herbs,
*and becometh a **tree**, so that the birds of the air*
come and lodge in the branches thereof.
~ Matthew 13:32 (King James Version) ~

Recently, a wise woman named Florence shared a bit of advice with me. She said some seeds must grow down first, establishing their roots, before they were ever able to break free topsoil from the dirt that's been covering them. She pointed out to me that not all people grow the same. It may appear they're not growing to the human or natural eye, only because we can't see all the changes taking place underneath the dirt their lives were once buried in. She told me just because the growth wasn't visible to our eyes, didn't mean there wasn't growth taking place. She also advised me of the importance of watching my words. She reminded me that for a seed to bring forth a good fruit, it needs the "good" words of the Son and rain of the Holy Spirit sprinkled over it DAILY to grow well. Hopefully I've heeded her advice in my life and in the writing of this book.

✐ [11]*Glory Cloud*
(2/07/03 – 12:43am)

Glory Cloud
Like a cloud of mercy misting out my mistakes
Glory Cloud
Like a window of love reflecting God's glorious Grace
Glory Cloud
Covering me with the power of Your Deity
Glory Cloud
Filling me to overflow supernaturally
Glory Cloud
Your Presence rains upon me abundantly
Glory Cloud
Delivering this captive and restoring liberty
Hmmm
Glory Cloud, yes I receive You

Okay so what is this "Home Grown" story all about? It's about freedom and liberation from a past that tries to keep you from reaching your future. Even as a young child who was being molested, I remember there were other demons that tried to come into my life to attack or attach themselves to me, like the spirit of homosexuality. Thank God, His Spirit was even then guarding me against submitting to that abomination.

---

[11]

Please let me clarify here because we all have own an individual opinion TODAY on sexual orientation or gender rights. Even our laws of the land have changed. So just because I choose to stand upon God's Word, does not mean I do not love or embrace my sister or brother who openly practice a lifestyle contrary to the Bible teaching. Yet for me, God's Word still stands as Truth. Sin is sin. This means that I likewise have to accept that I sinned by being promiscuous when I committed adultery in deed and thought. Sin is sin. One sin is no less or no greater than the other. My fornicating with others while married was a perversion before God. He clearly states this in Proverbs 5:1-23:

> [1]My son, if you listen closely to my wisdom and good sense [2]you will have sound judgment, and you will always know the right thing to say. [3]The words of an immoral woman may be as sweet as honey and as smoth as olive oil. [4]But all that you really get from being with her is bitter poison and pain. [5]If you follow her, she will lead you down to the world of the dead. [6]She has missed the path that leads to life and doesn't even know it. [7]My son, listen to me and do everything I say. [8]Stay away from a bad woman! Don't even go near the door of her house. [9]You will lose your self respect and end up in debt to some cruel person for the rest of your life. [10]Strangers will get your money and everything else you have worked for. [11]When it's all over, your body will waste away, as you groan [12]and shout, "I hated advice and correction! [13]I paid no attention to my teachers. [14]and now I am disgraced in front of everyone." [15]You should be faithful to your wife, just as you take water from your own well. [16]And don't be like a stream from which just any woman may take a drink. [17]Save yourself

for your wife, and don't have sex with other women. ^{18}Be happy with the wife you married when you were young. ^{19}She is beautiful and graceful, just like a deer, you should be attracted to her and stay deeply in love. ^{20}Don't go crazy over a woman who is unfaithful to her own husband! ^{21}The LORD sees everything, and he watches us closely. ^{22}Sinners are trapped and caught by their own evil deeds. ^{23}They get lost and die because of their foolishness and lack of self-control.

(Contemporary English Version - YouVersion).

By repenting 1 John 1:9, God saved me when I gave my life back over to Him. He redeemed, revived, refreshed, renewed and restored my life in 2015.

However, for me being born a female if I was to practice any unnatural behaviors defined in Romans 1:25-27, it would be perverse; especially if I was not born male, born transsexual or otherwise, as some clearly are in today's society. It is also clearly defined in the Bible what will befall those who practice without repentance these unnatural behaviors:

Romans 1:25-32

^{25}They exchanged the truth of God for a lie, and worshipped and served created things rather than the Creator--who is forever praised. Amen.
^{26}Because of this, God gave them over to shameful lusts. Even their women exchanged natural relations for unnatural ones. ^{27}In the same way the men also abandoned natural relations with women

and were inflamed with lust for one another.
Men committed indecent acts with other
men, and received in themselves the due
penalty for their perversion.
[28]Furthermore, since they did not think it
worthwhile to retain the knowledge of God,
he gave them over to a depraved mind, to
do what ought not to be done. [29]They have
become filled with every kind of wickedness,
evil, greed and depravity. They are full
of envy, murder, strife, deceit and malice.
They are gossips, [30]slanderers, God-haters,
insolent, arrogant and boastful; they
invent ways of doing evil; they disobey
their parents; [31]they are senseless, faithless,
heartless, ruthless. [32]Although they know
God's righteous decree that those who do
such things deserve death, they not only
continue to do these very things but also
approve of those who practice them.
(New International Version see www.
biblegateway.com)

Too often many victims of molestation or sexual abuse turn to one of these alternative lifestyles: promiscuity or homosexuality. This is **not** the will of God for our lives. We willingly abort **HIS** purpose for our lives when we give into these perversions.

HomeGrown is about learning from our past issues and mistakes so our children won't have to repeat them. It's about finding yourself and **loving who you are** in spite of what you've been. It's about becoming the person God has purposed you to be. Accept your past for the lessons it has taught you and then move confidently into who God designed for you to be before the foundations of this world came into being.

This book was ***not*** written to entertain you as a reader. Abuse is abuse and there's nothing at all entertaining about it. There are varying shades of it in every life, and for some its color boldly tries to darken its victims' entire being. But you and I have the power within to stop its darkness from spreading. It doesn't matter if the abuse was physical, mental, emotional or psychological. *HomeGrown* has been written to educate others of the plight of so many who are like me... and like you. They too got trapped in the secrecy of night rituals... that became the dark seeds of secret lives. It was written to say those secret seeds from our past can be buried and can still bring forth fruits of righteousness, when we bury them within the good ground of God's perfect love for us. Open up your life today and let His mercy and love and grace rain upon your heart and your soul. There's such peace and newness of life to be found in Him. There **is** rest in HIM for your weary soul. There is joy, unspeakable joy, in Jesus Christ. Don't be afraid anymore. God **is** your Protector. He's already been fighting for you. But you've got to be willing to make that first step towards freedom. Take His hand and keep your eyes focused on HIS Word. You've grown up past all of the hurt and the pain of what happened to you and you have survived. You're still here aren't you?

✐ [12]Rescue Me - From Me - Lord

(12/24,25/98 - 11:39pm to 12:02am)

Rescue me, not from sin
But rescue me Lord, from myself within

Rescue me; show me Your way
And tell me Jesus, for what I should pray

Rescue me Lord, my heart is so impure
Cleanse me and save me from me by
planting Your Word in my heart
Let Your Word take root deep within
and tears of sorrow and remorse
Wash away all sin

Rescue me from the spirits of pride and fear
Restore me unto You lord and draw me ever near

Rescue me and give me a testimony to share
To others lost in sin of Your loving care

Rescue me - from me - Lord Jesus
That I may glorify You with my life
And become a vessel for You to use to
Rescue others . . . from their worldly plights

When you've chosen to live a life contrary to the Word of God it does affect what happens in your life today. Don't compromise. So don't choose to become what you were not created to be. Learn to be who you truly are and don't be ashamed of who you were. Come into the light and out of the darkness... into your true home. Choose to live in freedom.

Get help by visiting some of the following websites and becoming informed about what's going on in your neighborhood, in your community. If you are a member of a good Bible-teaching church, get help from your ministry. If not, seek help from one or more of the sites listed below. They are various sites and resources you can contact for help when you've been a victim of abuse; to prevent abuse from happening to your child; for more information on abuse; or for to request counseling services or for someone to be in prayer with you:

http:icjax.com/
http://www.thepotterstouch.org/index.html
http:jmministries.org
http://www.isna.org/faq/transgender
http://www3.fdle.state.fl.us/sexual_predators/Search.asp?research=true
http://www.yellodyno.com/?source=overture
http://www.childmolestationprevention.org/index.html
http://www.enlightenedchoices.org/index.htm
http://www.childabuse.org/
http://www.onyourmind.net/
http://www.menderofhearts.com/services.htm

Thank you Minister Johnson, sir.

I am beyond honored that you would gift me with the right to use such a powerful testimony in my first, but praise God, not my last writing project for Him.

As you can see from the attached, I have placed your testimony on the end right before the final poem as the "PROLOGUE" to the entire Home Grown book. God has also moved upon my heart to add places or websites where those who may be still hurting can find help.

Again, thank you for the honor and privilege you've granted by entrusting me with a piece of your life's story. Together, I pray that our combined testimonies and deliverances through God's Anointed Power shall toll the freedom bell for many others who are still shackled in heart, mind and body through their entanglement with sin. I pray that whosoever God's shall direct to read or touch or hear about this writing shall be as the Son and truly be set free indeed!

God Bless!

Phasia
Your sister in Christ Jesus

[13]*Rain, The Water of Life*
(8/26/04 – 5:43pm)

The Bible tells us that God showers down rain on both the just and the unjust… or as the world likes to say "into every life some rain must fall". And since God rains His mercy and loving-kindness down upon us - our lives can't help but to become more fruitful and abundantly blessed with each rainfall. For where there is Living Water, there is Life.

13

Choose to live...

My Story – His Glory

Most of this poetry was written during a period in my life when I didn't know where I was headed. Over time, God keeps proving one thing to me over and over . . .

He will never leave me alone.
I take comfort and peace in this Truth.

Know that I didn't write this - the Holy Spirit wrote this - He is always alert and connected to the Word I've been blessed to receive despite my old natural sinful state. This is a Truth I am continually receiving, as I become more and more like Christ. God's Word says that I am a new creation (a new creature). When I accepted Jesus Christ in my life – I became born again. But I am learning that in order to remain victorious I must renew my soul – every moment of every day. Every day I must fight to keep the Light of God - my spirit man - supreme in my heart and over my life. Victory means more than just surviving – it means dominating! Dominating fear and uncertainty and depression, because I know that God's Word is true – He will never leave me nor forsake me. He will not, He will not, He will not give me up or let me go. I am most thankful for that promise of security and love. I am most thankful for Jesus Christ in my life.

This is therefore, my testimony - my story for His Glory.

My prayer has been (and still is) that my Lord and Savior Jesus Christ be continually magnified in my life every moment of every day. I am learning (sometimes in the midst of emotion-filled moments of life) that only in and through Jesus Christ shall I be victorious. Every day is a school day. I am sometimes the rebellious student, but He is always the patient Teacher. He loves me. In spite of me, He loves me and has promised to always love me. Yes, this is the history of my life but it is truly His story, created solely by and for Him to glorify Him. It is not about me; it's all about Him.

But who am I? I must admit I have not always been so obedient and so willing to let go of my own desires for God's will in my life. I kicked hard against the pricks. I wanted to glorify my memories and not God. I am learning... yes even now I am learning to trust God and not man. I have not always been so dependent upon His Love to succor me and give me strength. In beginning to understand Wisdom and God's Way, I am learning not to manipulate others or strive fruitlessly to have my own way. My best friend admonished me frequently for depending too heavily upon man and the arm of men to give me accolades and praise. It has taken some personal sacrifices of friendships along with gaining a more intimate and exact revelation from God's Word to show the truth of that admonishment to me. Thank you my friend. Through the pruning of God's Word, I am still learning that I am all that God is when the great "I AM" is inside of me.

Finally, I am even now being lovingly forced through His correction and yet firmly forced by man's rejection to lean on and to really learn about God. God's correction has confirmed to me that I am His child... for He disciplines those whom He loves. In retrospect, I see that man's rejection was really an act of Love, because what I thought was punishment and restrictive boundaries were actually meant for <u>my</u> good. They helped me really look for God in me (and in others). Each rejection was a shovel of dirt tossed on my selfish nature, burying that old me and allowing God's fresh new seed to grow unhindered in me. One very good friend once told me to find a way to rehearse this gift of poetry I've been given without allowing or depending upon emotional pain or challenges to push me into my God-given zone. This friend encouraged me to tell others of God's Love by meditating certain Old Testament scriptures and re-telling those stories again from the lady of that time's perspective. I was advised to learn just how much to release of myself to minister effectively to the spirit of others (and especially my husband) through God's written Word. Thank you my friend.

Finally but most of all, I want to thank my husband, Reggie. He did not leave me or forsake me even when I left him and forsook him. His heart and prayers were always with me ... covering me as God's Word commanded. I have learned that he is not perfect – but neither am I. We are however, in covenant – with each other and with God. And a rope of three shall not be easily broken.

As you read each poem and each counsel – let it shine a light in your heart and mind. With each new revelation, you'll see the darkness fleeing away from the Truth and you'll begin to see and know only the Truth. Rejoice! Rejoice in knowing that you are under "no condemnation" for there is no fear in perfect Love. I hope you are able to see the steps of transition from my own selfishness to God's righteousness in my heart and mind as you read. Some days dawn clearer and more Truth-filled than others do, and on some days I must search for the *rainbows through the clouds. But in these writings I am shown (and hopefully sharing) continually that <u>God is Perfect Love</u>. His plan for my life (and yours) is blessed, abundantly blessed. He is all around me and inside of me, so I persevere in looking for Him. He is the reason I live. At first this "poema" was written as therapy for me, but over time it evolved into tapestry of God's Love for me. His Love is woven into the life-blood of my heart. Every day He continues to show me reflections of His beauty in others. I see the beauty and fruitfulness of His seed grow and develop a strong foundation as I learn to humbly serve others. His Wisdom and Love was planted inside of me before I was birthed. The fruit of my life is His harvest.*

Therefore, I humbly say when you reach the end of my story – this is where you'll find His Glory.

Yes, this poema is more than testimonial – it is confessional. Each poem is an inward and outward purging of all that is not like God from me as I become more like the believer He fashioned me to be. Like silver is purified seven times in a vase of clay – likewise, the seed of life He plants inside of me purifies my inner heart through the fire of His Word. His forgiveness washes me clean seventy-times-seven.

My prayer *is that each day (with each poema you read); His Glory will pierce throughout (my life and yours) to shine like a rainbow until the life we live reflects Jesus. I pray that God's glory will highlight and uncover His blessed fruit of the Spirit – a treasure I now covet – deep inside of me and inside of you and draw it out. I pray that you shall hold fast to your confidence and reap the great compensations that God has in store for you as you go by faith on this painfully maturing and yet joyous journey.*

Let your story be repaired *by what you say about you. Why? Because God lives on the inside of you and when you tear down your life through sin, you are destroying the Zoë seed of*

God that the Greater One has planted on the inside of you for His Glory. When you open up your mouth – only let blessings flow forth. Face the demons trying to destroy your life and call forth the power of Jesus Christ to exorcise them. And do it with finality. Do it trusting God. Do it with faith in God that those demon-spirits too shall topple, as did the uncircumcised giant Goliath. As David slew Goliath with a smooth stone and a sling shot and then cut off his enemy's head – do the same to your enemy using the double-edged sword of the Word of God mightily and confidently as your weapon.

Who is this enemy you may be asking? Our enemy is not flesh and blood... but spiritual wickedness in high places. Your enemy (and mine) is anyTHING that tries to steal your love from God and cause your obeisance and attention to be distracted from Jesus Christ. As Deuteronomy 8 says . . . choose life. How do you do this? You water your spirit man daily with the Word so that it is full to overflowing with His precepts and promises. So when the pressure comes – and believe me, it shall come – you will have His promises to guide you, provide for you and direct you; to safeguard you, shelter you and comfort you. His Word is His promise.

Remind yourself . . . God's Word is a lamp unto your feet and a light unto your path. Whenever you begin to have doubt, focus on the Word.

It will grant you peace.

Have faith in the Word . . . for without faith it is impossible to please God. Learn to trust the Word.

It will grant you wisdom.

Remember that Faith cometh by hearing and hearing by

the Word of God – you cannot have faith without hearing the Word of God. You cannot truly hear the Word of God without receiving and watering a seed of faith. Learn to hear the Word.

It will grant you life.

In the beginning was the Word and the Word was with God and the Word was God. Faith comes by hearing God. Learn to obey the Word.

It will grant you joy.

So as you walk through the pages of your life... listen closely to – God . . . and hear – God . . . and receive – God... but more importantly – obey God. For obedience is better than sacrifice.

Finally, I pray for submission. Surrender totally and unconditionally. Don't hold 'nuthin' back. Stop trying to count the cost. Let God be God in your life and stop trying to be (as Joyce Meyer states) Holy Ghost Junior. God made each of us. He knows our frame. He knows and designed our purpose. He knows what's best for us. God knows your heart – He knows your thoughts even before you form them. Stop foolin' yourself (ya definitely ain't foolin' God). Be honest and be real with yourself and God. Surrender joyfully so you may gracefully be changed into God's glory. Finally, let God complete your story as you praise Him forevermore! And may God bless you.

Open up the pages of your life . . . and let God write history.

✒ [14]**The Burial of Selfishness**

(October '98)

Ladies and Gentlemen, Sistahs and Brothers . . . we gather here today to give our final remarks and to remember our dear departed friend "Selfishness".

We were all close friends with "Selfishness". There were days when we didn't leave home without our friend and loved one - Selfishness. But alas, "Selfishness" must now be laid to rest.

Sistah Humble, what do you recall about "Selfishness"?

Well, Brother Love, "Selfishness" was someone I was always compared against along with her brother "Pride". I was always told how amazing it was that we shared the same Father, being we were so vastly different in our spiritual outlook on life. "Selfishness" would always want to exert her own way with those around her. She hardly ever took "no" for an answer and when she did, it was always with her best interests in mind. I can't say I'm truly sorry that "Selfishness" is no longer here with us. Maybe now, Brother Pride will get a clearer picture of life and his role in it. But then our Father would always say, ". . . all things work together for the good according to His purpose . . .." - so Brother Love, we just have to be encouraged today.

What about you, Brother Pride? What do you remember and miss about Sistah Selfishness?

Well, Brother Love, you know that "Selfishness" and I were twins. I almost feel as if a part of me is now gone and rests in that dark, lonely grave with her. But you really want to know the truth? Half of the things she got all the credit for . . . well; I'm the one who actually did all the ground work. I mean, where would people be if I didn't give them the 'boost' in themselves that they so sorely need to make it in this life?

14

Without me, "Selfishness" was just a puppet anyway. We're all better off without her around to screw things up with her selfishness.

Well, we've heard from the family. Are there any friends that would like to give a final comment or eulogy on "Selfishness"?

Anyone got anything to add? (Brother Love looks around hopefully).

No . . . well, I guess she didn't leave here with too many friends. But then I'm not really surprised. Are you? After all, this is "Selfishness" we're burying here.

From ashes to ashes . . . and dust to dust . . . (scene fades out with Brother Love dropping imaginary sand on the coffin).

✎ ¹⁵Welcome To Earth
(October '98)

Welcome, welcome to this place!
Where we all participate in the rat race
In the beginning we all had it made
But Adam and Eve decided we all
needed to earn our daily bread
Cain killed Abel and started the homicide wheel a'turning
Now we all wish we were back in Eden
instead of headed towards a'burning
Welcome, welcome to this place!
Where kids kill kids, friends kill friends . . .
and parents kill their children
Some say just to be seen or heard
We all exclaim and react in wonder to what God
predicted from the beginning in His Word

15

We often say, "What is the world coming
to?" but if we really wanted to know
We would study the Bible more
We blame governments and teachers and
parents and friends and neighbors
Yet we refuse to accept the blame that's
parked at our own front door
Welcome, welcome to this place!
Where we are quick to give up on commitments . . .
saying its personal happiness we seek
We run from this one . . . to that one . . .
in search of the right one
But in this race we never quite discover
that God promised help-meet
We look for the answers on television
talkshows and national news
And we are never quite sure if we're the
ones using . . . or being used
Welcome, welcome to this place!
A land flowing with milk and honey . . . a land full of grace
A covenant found in the Bible not searching
the Internet and scanning cyberspace
Where are the opportunities of this land . . .
most times they seem so minute?
Or maybe they're there, but most are too
busy with self to really compute
Welcome, welcome to this place!
When was the last time you sang "Amazing Grace"?
Are we so shallow, we fail to see?
That without God's mercy, in hell is where we would be
Where are we headed in our search for a meaningful life?

Read the books of Jeremiah, Ezekiel, Daniel, 2
Timothy and Revelation for more Godly insight
Welcome, welcome to this place!
America - It's the land God has given us for a price
The life of His Son . . . and my Savior - Jesus Christ!

✐ ¹⁶God Will Never Leave Me Alone
(12/24/98 - 10:39pm)

What, Lord, would You have me to do?
Help me to understand Your will for my life.
I feel so lost and alone, but I know You are waiting.
Waiting . . . Waiting . . ..

Help me to feel Your Presence.
Comfort me now Lord with Your strength
Guide me dear Jesus out of this darkness
Loosen up the chains I have been bound by

Father, You have said in Your Word
". . . be anxious for nothing . . .." Anchor me in Your Word
Help me, dear Lord, to seek You . . .
To seek You . . . to seek . . . seek You, Father

Help me to know and understand You are here . . .
Always here, waiting for me to reach out to You Father God
Fill me with Your loving Spirit of joy and peace
Fill me with Your comforting Spirit of mercy

Teach me Lord, Your way.
Be unto me a Friend when I feel abandoned and without hope
Restore the joy of my salvation in Your Presence
Bring to my remembrance Your abundant blessings unto me

Mature me in Your Truth.
Help me to believe in Your promises
and to stand upon Your Word.
Knowing and believing, whole-heartedly that
God will never leave me alone.

✐ [17]Rescue Me – From Me – Lord

(12/24,25/98 - 11:39pm to 12:02am)

Rescue me, not from sin
But rescue me Lord, from myself within

Rescue me; show me Your way
And tell me Jesus, for what I should pray

Rescue me Lord, my heart is so impure
Cleanse me and save me from me by
planting Your Word in my heart
Let Your Word take root deep within
and tears of sorrow and remorse
Wash away all sin

Rescue me from the spirits of pride and fear
Restore me unto You lord and draw me ever near

---

[17]

Rescue me and give me a testimony to share
To others lost in sin of Your loving care

Rescue me - from me - Lord Jesus
That I may glorify You with my life
And become a vessel for You to use to
Rescue others . . . from their worldly plights

✒ 18Lead Me Father

(12/25/98 - 12:05am)

Lead me Father, I am too lost to know the right way
Blinded by uncertainties, guide me O'Father with Your Word
Weakened by fears, gird me God Jehovah
with a renewed faith in Jesus
Strength.
I know You are there, one step - one
letter - away from being "here"
Please give me patience to bear, not the
yoke of sin, but the tears . . .
the tears . . ..
Thank You Jesus. Praises be unto Jesus, Hallelujah!
Help me to lift my spirit up in praises to You
Lord and break the chains of slavery
It's in the Praise!
Healing
Strength
Joy
Peace
Hope

Courage

Love

Lead me Father into Your gates with thanksgiving and praise

Lead me, Lord Jesus into You.

✐ ¹⁹Obedience Is . . .

(12/25/98 - 11:35pm)

. . . better than sacrifice or insincere offerings

. . . better than riches, fame or worldly gains

. . . a walk of faith in an uphill battle

. . . a blessing to those who are - obedient to God

✐ ²⁰Grace and Mercy

(12/25/98)

I ran across some old friends the other day - Grace and Mercy. You know, they told me where all they had been lately: In bars - rescuing the drunks from DUI convictions and deaths . . . In hotels - rescuing runaways from a life of prostitution and drug additions . . .

In hospitals - rescuing patients from disease and terminal illnesses . . . In jails - bringing salvation and hope to the prisoners. But you want to know what really amazed me about where they had been?

In my life . . . rescuing me from myself!

You know, they told me about my buddy . . . You know "who" - Temptation. Grace and Mercy said they saw the ways

---

19

20

and many times Temptation would say, "Aw, just take one muscle relaxant - you need the rest and after all it's not as if you're abusing your body with drugs. I mean, you do have a prescription don't you?" Or Temptation would convince me a friendship with this or that married man was harmless. C'mon Phasia, it's just an innocent lunch. I mean, it's not as though it's a date or anything - you guys are just friends. So what if he's making calf eyes at you and his compliments make you feel special - it's all harmless. I mean you are a married woman. And boy, would Temptation really blind-side me with pride and selfishness. At work, my lack of delegation and attitude that if I didn't do the job, it would never be done properly were all rooted in a weed called perfectionism. And Grace and Mercy were quick to point out that only our Lord and Savior Jesus Christ is perfect. Grace and Mercy then pointed out that drugs and sex do have their place in our lives. Drugs should be prescribed and the prescription should only be used to treat an illness or ailment. And sex is a gift give to us by our Heavenly Father . . . to enjoy and share in a marriage-covenant relationship. But selfishness and pride - well, Grace and Mercy could only advise me that they be plucked up like the weeds they are growing to choke out my life.

Grace and Mercy also assured me that any remnants would be wiped clean from the slate of my life upon repentance and confession to God as another gift of His unmerited favor and His unending daily blessings to me. As Christian author McKinney Hammond stated in "The Genius of Temptation", "how do we crawl out from under the wet blanket of condemnation? How do we regain our confidence and get back in a justified position? - Repent! And then - Let us come boldly to the throne of our gracious God - really meaning business with him like we

do with Uncle Sam. There, we will - to be sure- receive
His mercy, and we will find grace to help us when we
need it . . . - And then - continue to live in fellowship
with Christ so that when He returns, you will be full of
courage and not shrink back from Him in shame. And
just to show me who my true friends were, Grace and
Mercy gave me some advice through this author's writing
on how to escape the deadly traps of Temptation:

(1) Stop, and carefully ponder the matter or "Selah"
(2) Before sampling any of those delectable looking treats
being waved beneath the sensory outlets - consider the
costs. No hors d'oeuvre is really for free.
(3) Remember finally,

Grace is being given something good we don't deserve.
Mercy is not being given our just desserts.

This author also paraphrased, "Grace is when you go
'Wow!' and Mercy is when you wipe your brow and go, 'Whew!'"
I just want to get past the "Whew!" and graduate to the "Well
done, my good and faithful servant . . . Well done."

✐ [21]Going Through The
Motions - Isaiah 29:13,14
(12/26/98 - 11:30am)

Why would you give to the hungry an empty bowl?
Why would you give to the thirsty vinegar to drink?
Why offer praises to God that other men might see?

21

Why would you be a Pharisee?
Who is the Potter that makes the clay?
Who is the Anointed One who died on Calvary that day?
Who is the God known as the great I AM?
Do you truly believe on Jesus?
God's Sacrificial Lamb
(or are you running a scam?)
Where are the hypocrites?
Are they in church or congregated without?
Know they not - there is no hiding spot
Almighty God sees all our deeds
Confessed or not
Shall the musician not know his own composition?
Shall the florist not recognize his own arrangement?
Shall the mathematician not be able
to solve his own formula?
Shall God not know, recognize and solve
the problems of His own creation?
In Psalms 139:23,24 - God says He searches me and He
tries me and He knows if there be any wicked way in me . . .
Isaiah 29:15,16 God shows how hypocrisy
will blind those who think they see
These will never realize that if they are
merely going through the motions
A child of God they will never be

✐ ²²**Touch Me**

(12/26/98 - 12:20pm)

Touch me Lord Jesus
With Your Spirit
In my spirit
Help me to feel Your Presence
Deep within
Give me a discerning heart
To know Your voice
Whenever You speak to me
Open my spiritual ears
And let me listen
And obey
With my whole soul.

✐ ²³**A Tie That Binds - Isaiah 52 & 53**

(12/26/98 - 12:28pm)

Cleansed by His grief-stricken tears
Forgiven, despite our wrongs year by year
Touched with a Spirit of Peace
Thank You Father - for a tie that binds
Bruised for our iniquities
Wounded for our transgressions
Scorned by those He hath redeemed
Thank You Father - for a tie that binds
Healed because of stripes He beared
Justified because of righteousness He shared

22

23

Offered as a living sacrifice - my sins He cleared
Thank You Father - for a tie that binds
Jesus Christ . . . a tie that binds

✎ 24Island of Patmos

(12/26/98 - 7:48pm @ Devin's)

Child of God - what island are you isolated upon?
From where have you allowed Satan to cut you off?
O Sinner man - O sinner woman - do you not know
that God's moat of protection flows all around you?
Child of God - what shelters you from Satan's snare?
Where do you hide from worldly cares?
Seek ye first the Kingdom of God and His righteousness . . .
And His word shall be the drawbridge of
escape from your island of patmos.

✎ 25Stop Mooning The World

(12/26/98 - 8:45pm @ Devin's)

Let God cover you with righteousness
Stop mooning the world with your sins
Let God's word cover you with knowledge
Stop mooning the world with your ignorance
Let God cover you with His spirit of peace
Stop mooning the world with your chaos
Take off your straight jackets and put on your physician's coat

---

24

25

Stop mooning the world and let God
show you how to heal thyself

✍ 26**Appearances**
(12/27/98 - 11:30pm @ Lena's)

Who are we, and are we who we appear to be?
Why do we pretend?
Do we seek to impress friends?
Friends would never need a façade
They take you as you are made
With true friends, you can be real
And show how you truly feel
There is no need to hide
They know what you feel inside
So why do we put on appearances?
Don't we know they can never truly cover
the pain hidden within us?
They are like foundational powders
That wash off with our tears
And they never, ever allow us to be real

✍ 27**Sean**
(12/27/98 - 12am @ Lena's)

A complexity filled with dreams
A dreamer who is not what he seems
A smile full of light

26

27

Who is this drummer - this Shilite?
A friend without excuse
A musician in God's use
Who can fathom this man called Sean
One of God's notes in His symphony

✐ 28**Purged!**
(12/28/98 - 2:18pm)

Like the sweetness of chocolates filled with creme
I crave a taste of you
Like the relief of a massage
I feel your touch
O wretched soul am I
Purge me Lord, lest I die!
Like the flame of a wildfire
I feel your heat
Like the softness of fog
You cover my thoughts like a sheet
(blinding me . . . blinding me)
O wretched soul am I
Purge me Lord, lest I die!

✐ 29**Choices Made Me**
(01/30/99 - 7:30pm)

We have no choice to whom we are born
But we are given the choice to conform or be transformed

28

29

We have no choice in being born male or female
But God gives us the choice of expanding our minds
and becoming all that we can be in Christ Jesus
We have no choice in our sisters or brothers of birth
But God grants us a family built and
grounded in His Holy Word
For He chose us first
When I think back over the choices I have
made in this life I realize that
Choices made me

✒ 30**For the Moment - or for eternity?**
(01/30/99 - 7:35pm and 03/25/02 – 4:55pm)

Freedom, do I define as being happy
for the moment or for eternity?
Wisdom, do I define as making decisions for the moment?
Or for eternity?
Listen to God, not man
Let God's Wisdom be your guide
Open up the Bible and free the shackles off your mind
Only then will you capture moments of time in eternity

✒ 31**To Say Yes**
(01/30/99 - 7:40pm)

To say yes would compromise all that I
am and strive to be . . . in Christ

30

31

To say yes would erase God out and let ego
keep me from being . . . in Christ
To say yes would leave a fleshly legacy and my spirit would
no longer find a dwelling place . . . in Christ
To say yes would be to sign a death warrant for
me and my child to all that we have inherited
from Abba, our Father . . . in Christ
So I have chosen to say no.

✐ ³²**Carissa**

(01/20/99 - 7:50pm)

So full of joy and life
A rainbow casting light from above
So friendly and open to others
An inquisitive puzzle full of answers
So confident and self-possessed
A child learning about Godliness

✐ ³³**STAND**

(01/30/99 - 8pm)

S Stay spiritual   **S** Study God's Word daily
T Test all spirits   **T** Trust God always
A Answer to God's Word   **A** Act on the Word of God
N Never stop hoping   **N** Never quit trying
D Depend on God   **D** Deliverance is in the
                                                       praise!

32

33

✎ [34]No Substitutes

(01/31/99 - 9:15pm @ Eddie's)

There are times when I yearn for your touch
Times when I cry for your voice in my ear
There are times when my body aches to feel you inside me
But there are no substitutes
There are times when I remember the
special urgency of your desire
Times when I taste the softness of your lips upon mine
There are times when my eyes dream of
seeing yours every morning and night
But there are no substitutes
I search for you in the eyes of others
I seek your feel by touching another
But there are no substitutes
There are no "earthly" substitutes

✎ [35]Questions to Ask Yourself

(01/31/99 - 10:30pm)

Why do we share painful experiences?
Why do we ask questions that have no rational answers?
Why do we seek fulfillment in man instead of God?
Why?
Do we search for someone who cares
by the level of pain inflicted?
Do we blind ourselves to God's blessings by
focusing upon our circumstances?

34

35

Do we forget we are children of God who must
nourish the Spirit and not the flesh?
Do we know?
What good are regrets in a life that's been spent?
What good are promises that are impossible to keep?
What good is love that is not heaven sent?
What good are these?

✐ 36**Blessed**
(01/31/99 - 10:45pm)

Blessed spiritually, even when I was poor materially
Blessed physically, tongue to taste, eyes
to see, ears to hear, hands to write
Count thee the ways

✐ 37**Power Trip**
(02/01/99 - 12:30am)

Unbeliever . . .
Calculated by Satan to rule out all common sense
Manipulated by flesh to take pride in compliments
Titillated by man's vain nonsense
Irritated by sin's never ending persistence
Complicated by selfish desires
Believer . . .
Arbitrated for by the blood of Jesus
Regulated by the Word of God

36

37

Regenerated by the Holy Spirit
Elevated and escalated by thankfulness and praise
Dedicated to the Holy Trinity
Forever . . .
Lord God let my trip be towards the
filling of your Holy power
Taking hope and courage from knowing you care

✐ [38]**Be Mine**

(02/02/99 - 10:40pm)

Thank You Lord for being my strength
When I am weak
Thank You Lord for being my light
When I am in darkness
Thank You Lord for being my guide
When I am blind
Thank You Lord for being my joy
When I am in sorrow
Thank You Lord for being my hope for all the tomorrows

✐ [39]**Untitled Prayer**

(02/05/99 - 1:50am)

Lord Jesus, I don't want the chastisement
Lord Jesus, I prefer the advisement
Thank You for Your Holy Word!

---

[38]

[39]

✐ ⁴⁰Disconnected (or wrong number)

(02/13/99 - 11:54am)

When we sin, we breach our connection to God

Lord Jesus help me to disconnect from the things of this world, things holding me back from establishing a clear, strong connection with you

Lord Jesus help me to hang up the connection from all desires, be they within or without and call upon you

Lord Jesus help me to become disconnected from lustful flesh and connected to love for Christ

Lord Jesus help me to become disconnected from sinful thoughts and connected to spiritual things

Lord Jesus help me to become disconnected from fear and connected to faith

Lord Jesus help me to become disconnected from pride in self and connected to praise to God

Lord Jesus help me to become disconnected from myself and connected to Jesus Christ again

Amen

✐ ⁴¹Untitled Truth

(02/13/99 -12:18pm)

What can wash away my sins?
Nothing but the blood of Jesus
What can make me whole again?
Nothing but the blood of Jesus

40

41

🖋 [42]Psalm of Reverence

(March 2001 - written for Minister Reese's Layman II class)

Hungering daily for Your Presence Lord
I find You here - always near
Keeping Your promise never to leave or forsake me
Craving eternally for Your touch
You flow over me like a heart-rending symphony
Filling my spirit, soul and body with Your harmony
Overwhelmed
My whole being bows down in worship to Your Presence
Acknowledging Your Grace - proclaiming Your Mercy
Yearning intensely for Your pleasure
I joyously give thanks as I embrace Your Holy Spirit
As rivers of water flow over rocks smoothing away all edges
So are my heart strings steadily washed
and purified by Your Word
Into a beautiful composition
Resounding Your Peace
Flooded and overflowing with Your Love
Seeking diligently for Your Wisdom
I AM . . . i am
Covered by the Blood of Jesus Christ
Blessed
All of my needs are met past overflow
Given the honor to boast of Your Righteousness
Royalty?
Yes, I walk in divine authority
Priestly?
Yes, I am submitted and compassionate
Always - I am Your child God

---

[42]

For I am designed to worship You
I am perfected to Praise

✐ [43]Here In My Heart . . . (inspired by Isaiah 55:1-6)

(2/7/01 – 12:54am)

Here in my heart
I make the choice
To recognize and heed His Voice

No more confusion
Strife, stress and pain
Only to walk in Jesus' name

I will concede
Unto His will
To walk in love and harmony
I recognize
I am His child
For me He hung His head and died

(slower tune . . . stretching. . . different rhythm)
Holy Trinity . . . Holy Spirit within
Gave me new life and freedom from sin
He paid the price – One Sacrifice
He paid the price . . . to set me free

I am renewed
Your vessel to use

43

Lord use me to set the captives free
(Repeat)

Here in my heart
I make the choice
To recognize and heed His Voice

Walking in love
Not fortune or fame
Only to glorify Jesus' Name

Here in my heart
I make the choice
To recognize and heed His Voice

Walking in love
No glory I claim
Only to magnify His Holy Name

Jesus our Lord
You who rose from the grave
Come let us worship His Blessed Name

Jesus my Lord
I make the choice
To recognize and heed Your Voice

No money I bring
Lord only Your Name
Supplies and fulfils my every need

So I seek You Lord
While You may be found,

'Cause in You does love and grace abound

So here in my heart
I make the choice
To recognize and heed Your Voice

Show me Your way
Lord use me like clay
My only desire is to obey
To walk in Your will
Your purpose fulfilled
As I witness to the world of Your goodwill

I surrender myself
I shall pass the test
With new life in Christ
I am eternally blessed

I am renewed
Your vessel to use
Lord use me to set the captives free
(Repeat)

✐ 44Stop Feeling Sorry For Yourself and Be Empowered

(3/14/01 – 12:38am)

Please do not assume that just because I am a black female
living in Florida that I voted for Al Gore – I do not assume
you live in a shotgun house with a 3rd grade education

44

Certain rules and regulations only tend to foster
more resentment that creates more discrimination
and breeds more lack . . . in blacks . . . lack of self-
esteem, lack of education, lack of empowerment, lack
of creativity, lack of opportunity and a lack of trying

Many people (low-income blacks and whites particularly)
do not know they are the object of discrimination until
some "power broker" trying to build a political platform
comes along and decides points it out – for their benefit

Why do blacks (intelligent blacks) say that we are playing on
an unfair playing field that only Affirmative Action can level?

Blacks need to become more involved and stop being
so apathetic – Become **pro**active and not so **re**active

EVERY PERSON HAS THE POWER TO CHANGE a
situation but it begins by first deciding to allow yourself to
be changed – each person has a CHOICE to use that power

Why do folks, especially black folks, indiscriminately
jump on the bandwagon of rebel rousers and high-
profile groups when the fanfare is up high?

Why is the glory and limelight the draw? Get real
people! The only One who should ever be glorified is
Jesus Christ – not a man, no man is more different or
more gifted than you are. You need to know who you
really are and step out into YOUR opportunities

Stop being so ignorant! Educate yourselves! Stop
letting yourself be taken advantage of by others,
especially by high-powered Blacks (and Whites) who
are only looking for a platform to increase their own
popularity, political profile or financial foundation

LEARN HOW TO PRAY. Stop being a prey! Stop allowing
yourselves to be used. Stop pretending. Empower yourself.
Fight for yourself and you will be fighting for others who
are just like you through race, nationality or gender

RENEW YOUR MIND ... really dig deep inside of you
and find the SPIRIT that guides and comforts you and
leads you to your ideal best – EXPAND YOUR FAITH

Break out of your cycle of being oppressed and EACH ONE
REACH ONE with a word of hope – help someone else
(somebody helped you! Whether you acknowledge it or not)

Stand up and decide to make the
difference, otherwise – SHUT UP!

✎ 45Untitled Lyrics

(08/31/01 - 1:30am on phone w/ Nita - written for Firestorm)

Get into this
Shed your inhibitions
It's for you; it's for me
It's worship unto God
Be on one accord (there's integrity there)

45

Experience God
Let the experience blow you away
Blow away all your cares

✐ [46]**Freedom Reigns**
(09/18/01 – 11:30am)

Freedom reigns in this place . . . a land
filled with God's mercy and grace
The sacrifice of lives . . . that some made . . . of
others taken . . . some saved . . . some lost
For you – Jesus Christ paid the final price at the cross
Psalms 91:16 declares "with long life will He satisfy me
(America) and show me His salvation (deliverance)"
Pray for the souls that remain to be saved . . .
as the battles continue to rage
As a nation we'll stand for freedom and fight for liberty
Americans . . . stand in Unity
Patriotic . . . flags wave . . . support our leaders
Faithful . . . prayers raised . . . rejoice for the Victory to come
Call to arms Faith in the Holy God
to lead us in an unholy war
(already won)
Let Freedom Reign!

---

[46]

✐ [47]Advice 4 U & I

(10/14/01 – 6:59pm)

Nita, The counsel of the Lord says "don't run away, stay connected to the ministry I've been called to... Stay, cleave, and serve. The Word called at me today from so many different sources and from such a wide range of directions, but it (they) all convalesced into the same Word. Commit. Minister Cooper spoke this.... "you're in the place where God is manifesting blessings. Press in further, don't run or retreat. Don't let the devil or tricks of the enemy push you away. Endure, press in and put your faith to the test and see God's glory manifested in your life. Stay hooked up to the anointing". Pastor Crawford spoke this.... "A lot of times we knock down the challenges in our lives, (like David and Goliath) but we don't cut the head off - making sure that issue or challenge will not rise again. Make sure you kill that thing and preserve and protect your life and the lives of those Anointed ones you serve". Minister Davis spoke this.... "1. Know yourself - really know yourself. 2. Cast down imaginations and build up your immune systems with the Word of God. Learn how to protect yourself from everything except for what I've come to receive from God. Cut off those ungodly soul ties. Deal with the situations. 3. Cut off the past - TOTALLY! 4. Know your boundaries - be honest to yourself. 5. Make sure you're not drawing from anyone else - emotionally - outside of God (or your spouse). Find out exactly what you feel you are getting from others that you are not getting from your significant other and discern why. 6. Find out how you can receive this from your current "safe" circle of friends. 7. Be held accountable to a godly, honest friend who will keep your feet to the path of God without compromise.

---

[47]

⌀ [48]Friends stand together . . .
Nita and Monica
(10/16/01)

This is what we're up against. Here's both the prayer and the answer. I shall not run this time. I will obey. I shall not allow Satan to take any good thing God has for me away or cause me to abort His Blessings, which are even now flowing my way. The river of God shall only be Quickened within me and my spirit is even now flowing on track. I have already been delivered. I shall STAND.

⌀ [49]Words from my Elizabeth
(10/16/01 – 1:17pm)

You know that I am just about in tears. I love you so much and know that this is a very critical time in your life and a very vulnerable and sensitive one. I know that God is ordering your steps. The enemy is also throwing rocks in the path. The blood of Jesus is against him. Baby girl, you did not come this far to stop now. The house has been swept but it is not filled so the enemy will come back w/ 7 more demons. I don't think so. We are watchmen on the wall and I know there are things we do that are very innocent but b/c the flesh wants affirmation it will receive it from whomever and wherever. You see as women we have this tendency to take what we can get even if it's not for the long haul and then we are left broken and in despair and discontented. You deserve ALLLLL nothing less and I prophesy over your life

---

48

49

that your life is filled with the abundance of God and there is no lack. All you need has been prepared in the spiritual and I command that is made manifest with the love of your life the man that covers you and comforts you and affirms you Reginald. The father of your child, the hello in your morning. The flutters in your stomach. Yes, God made no mistake and you are not a failure there is nothing wrong with you for you are in the making and in order for there to be a filling the nasty and defiled things have to be removed to make provision for the good stuff. You are fearfully and wonderfully made and God DON'T make mistakes. You hear me. So let joy arise and know that if you make one step God will make two. Put off anything that will keep you tied to anything that looks like your past. Declare your future to be nigh thee even in your mouth. You are precious to God and He loves the clay that HE is making. Be strengthened and do the things that you dare to do if you want to see the new things and fulfillment you prematurely experienced.

Break forth for the time is now. I love you. . . . Nita

✐ 50There Is No Substitute . . .

(10/17/01 – 11:15pm)

Are you okay? No, I'm so far away it's not even funny. I'm past, way past being NOT okay. Talk to me. Save me! The sand is flowing quick, I'm at the point of being dragged beneath its muddy depths. Save me Father. My hand is outstretched. Please Father, Save me – rescue me – from me.

My spirit man desires to please only You – my flesh, defiant flesh, lives for this moment only in idolatry. Flirting with words,

---

50

teasing with innuendoes – we're headed on a rushing river of desire to nowhere. Nowhere, because You're not there. Your Presence is totally absent from the path of unrighteousness that beckons so invitingly. My carnal senses scream for release and satisfaction – to take a nibble, a bite and then totally devour that tempting morsel of flesh. I long and I ache and the thread of reason grows more and more thin. Intoxicating is the Presence of Your Spirit O Lord. Invigorating is the temptation. The tug of war grows more and more fierce.

Help me Father God! Please help me. I cannot do this on my own. I am too weak. Be my Strength. Complete me; be made perfect in me. Cool the burning fires of desire and the wretched addition of adulation. Open my eyes – let me see. Let me see clearly the pathway of destruction, which yawns open hungrily for the unwary, the slack, those not standing guard diligently. Cleanse me. Purify me. Let the sin sweat out of my pores and refresh me with Your Word. Hear Your servant, Your child, and Your princess. I declare I am righteous. I declare I am Holy. I declare I am More Than A Conqueror. I purpose to stand steadfast and unmovable always abounding in the Word of the Lord. Swamp me in Your cloak of protection – Surround me with Your Love. Shelter me during this storm. Bring me forth as a vessel pure and without blemish. Remove all the wax so my imperfections are clearly visible to me. Show me how to heal. Numb my body to sin's hook and anesthetize my heart. Cleanse me. Cleanse me. Cleanse me . . . Cleanse . . . me . . . Clean . . . m . . ..

✍ 51**The Battle . . .**

(10/17/01 – 11:40pm)

. . . is real. Touch not mine Anointed saith the Lord of Hosts. Raise not thine hand against mine child. Fear not, for I am with thee. Maintain and have Patience. Seek My Strength in your time of weakness. Know that I shall not let you fall. I shall not abandon you to the devourer. Hold fast. Do not relax your guard when the fire gets hotter and the Pressure becomes intense. Know that I have Chosen you. You are Mine. He desires to have you – to complete what he began before BUT I will not, I will not, I will not give you up. STAND for my reward stands before you even now. Release NOT your faith. Hold firm to your Call. I will uphold you, as Aaron and Hur upheld Moses, you shall be victorious IF you trust Me and know I AM all that I say I Am. Just obey Me. Let Me show you the true way – Come home into ME. Do not give . . ..

✍ 52**The Birth is . . .**

(10/18/01 – 12:05am)

. . . imminent, don't abort. PUSH. I shall not leave you. I will cover you. You shall not go through this fire alone. But you shall come out strong. Trust ME. ONLY Me. I have never lied to you – and I never shall.

51

52

✐ 53I Love You, . . . Your Dad
(10/18/01 – 12:14pm)

Do not fear giving away too much information. Surround
yourself with friends and loved ones who have MY best
interests at heart. Keep a step ahead of the enemy by
unarming all of his potential weapons against you. Yes,
tell the other one what I have said – it is for him too.
You both need to be focused on Me. I will succor you.
Do not be concerned about what other people may think
or say – just know that I have blessed your covenant
of anointing, of favor. Know that I am with you both
separately and together and no one shall snatch you
out of Mine Hand. I love you. I Love you. I love You.

✐ 54The Way of Success
(10/18/01 – 1:48pm)

Rejection is only the catalyst to success
Rejection propels us to try harder and OVERCOME all odds

✐ 55Phasia . . . There Are No Substitutes
(10/22/01 – 6:45pm)

There are times when I yearn for your touch
Times when I cry for your voice in my ear
There are times when I can hear the sound of your smile

53

54

55

But there are no substitutes

Times when I imagine the softness of your lips upon mine
There are times when my eyes dream of
seeing yours every day and night
There are times when my love aches to touch your life
But there are no substitutes

I search for you in the eyes of others
I seek your feel by touching another
Searching in vain trying to remove this pain filled void
But there are no substitutes

Baby Girl – I need you – please open your eyes and see
You are – in this life – the biggest part of me
To my heart you hold the key
4 U . . .
There are no substitutes

✐ 56W.O.W.

(10/27/01 – 8:30am – after reading the Amp.
Version of the book of Titus)

Yes my Lord, I shall rest and abide in You – constantly
drawing my strength from You, only You. I shall continue to
seek Your Presence to bask in the awesome wonder of Your
Love and Peace, Your Joy and Wisdom. A sound MIND is
my reward, ya ha ha ha – it is mine. Obedience is the key,
have I not told you this before; yes, you are on your way – do
not stray and know if you should lose sight of the way – close

---

56

your physical eyes and let ME reveal to your spiritual heart
MY will and MY plan which is even now manifesting, which
is even now in covenant with my men of God – your Husband
first, your Pastor next and then your mentor Minister Davis –
yea, Tanyita is your Elizabeth, she will exhort, advise and
encourage you. She will not abandon you. There are others,
but these are the keys to your poetry. AMEN. So Be It.
(… 1 Peter 5:8 … Minister Reese at Prayer concluded
by saying "do it more intensely, be sober and know we
have the authority to make sure victory is manifested")

✐ 57...**For The Moment**
(11/19/01 – 4:45pm)

Our flesh is never promised tomorrow
All <u>our</u> dreams are hinged on yesterday
Our love will always be strong today... for the moment

Though our hearts are full of sorrow
And the path forward may seem unclear (and hollow)
Our love will always be strong today... for the moment

Yes, the tears well up and overflow
Hands, bodies and minds will not to let go
Our love will always be strong today... for the moment

Each moment is now... it stands alone
So we'll let go and learn to be strong
Right here... right now... for the moment

57

You may delete my Word from your sight
My love for you shall not depart
You shall remain in my heart
Right here... right now... eternally... for the moment

✐ ⁵⁸Help!

(01/25/02 – 1:00am)

Listening to the tape from last night's service really convicted me. I know what the Word of God says - cast not away your confidence which has great recompense of reward but have patience.... I am not sure if I'm traveling the right road. I want to have what I had before "yesterday". I want my Joy back. I want my Peace back. I want my Praise back. I want my Strength in Jesus back. How do I get back to "there"? I want to be in HIS presence again, with no inhibitions and no hindrances. No guilt and no shame. How did you get back there? I still hear from God. I know He speaks to me. I've even made a public and humbling acknowledgement before others, yet I still feel a sense of disconnection. What am I missing? I spend time with God in person - have I not dug deep enough? I don't feel as "Filled" with the Holy Ghost and I know His heart presence is missing. Do I, as Pastor exhorts "stir myself up"? Have my own "praise party". Maybe, yes, that's it. Right now I feel like Pastor is talking about me everytime he mentions something about not letting my past come up to ruin or destroy my today or my tomorrow. I feel like there is a dark cloud hanging over me, waiting to dump doom and pain and stuff out on me. Each of these days when I feel like this is a battle. I listen to the Word day in and day out and I still feel like I'm missing it. I am about at the end of my rope. I feel like a "Martha", a weary warrior and fainting saint (to borrow a Joyce Meyer book title). Should I even be asking you for help? But who else can I turn to? I know God is there, but... My husband wouldn't want to know even if I wanted to tell him... Some things can't even be shared with girlfriends, especially if you kept certain things from them to start with.... I haven't written this much since ... I don't even know the last time I wrote this much. (And looking back over what I've written, maybe it's a good thing too) Not making journal entries or any other creative writings. Maybe I need a "get away day to spend with God and I alone". You know, it's not like any other person is worth losing my salvation over. I know this. I truly do. I've been studying and I know that some shall fall away - I have declared I shall not be one of those, but I must admit sometimes I'm not so sure anymore. God knows my heart and I wish He would show me and deliver me from this pain. This pain of separation I feel so keenly from Him in this time ... like now. There are moments when I feel His presence but those moments are faint and almost ethereal. Like wisps. I need contact. I need His love to wash over me and cleanse me. I cry out for His presence. I want and I need His presence. It's like I work or stay busy to keep from feeling and thinking and reacting and acting. God told me to "SLOW DOWN" or risk "MISSING MY MOMENT FOR GOING TOO FAST". So I thought. I won't run out and get another job. I'll apply for Unemployment Compensation. This time, I'll wait on God. I'll tarry. I'm not sure I've been doing that. I'm not sure of much anymore. God is telling me things. Supernatural Miraculous things - this I know cause He is confirming it to others in my presence in my circle of associates. I am truly the clay. He is working and shaping me. I am on His work shelf, crying to get off and yet afraid I'm not ready. After the Tim Storey message last Friday, I don't want to jump off without being ready or released and fall into a flame that causes me to lose it all or worst - destroys me. What exactly am I seeking? Am I seeking HIS will? Am I seeking my own? I've always thought, even as a child, that I would be rich and famous when I grew up. Now all those who are rich AND famous aren't truly happy - if you believe everything you read and hear on the news. Have I grown up yet? I feel lately that I am just a baby. A big selfish baby. It's like I want to be mature and I want to be humble, but I'm caught in my own trap of being more... More... More... I need to be less to be more. Maybe I'm too caught up in all that I think I have accomplished. This time is a humbling time. Being taken down a peg and being denied is humbling. I pray that God is being perfected in me right now as I seek answers; His will – His way – His plan – His end. I desire that my latter be greater than the rest, my past. I desire that His wisdom will overshadow me and guide me. I desire to be the apple of His eye. I desire HIM. Sometimes I wish I were already there with Him. But that's pure selfishness speaking out again.

So...

I know we are not close anymore. I only now just realized exactly what was lost by bounds being overstepped. I pray that some areas can be restored - Godly areas. I needed to talk but maybe this is better. I don't feel comfortable around you much anymore. Too much - Lost. Too much – Given. It's like I'm numb and all feeling is capped up and put away in a storage room. Don't get me wrong, I feel anger and pity and sadness and tiredness and remorse. I feel regret for getting so close that I almost dishonored you and your position in my life. I don't want to hurt Jesus again. I've been unfaithful so many times and He has always been there. He has never let me go - even when I pushed away from Him. So the distance is necessary (for me) while I regain my balance. It's coming. It's almost here. Got it (smile).

How far do you go trying to convince yourself everything is alright? Until you believe it? God truly does know the heart and He is laying mine bare right now. It's not a pretty sight. I don't want to be like Esau, craving a momentary physical satisfaction at the cost of mine heavenly inheritance. You know what's really strange? I really thought I had it all together before yesterday – No condemnation. It's just that I thought that I had it all together. Maybe that was my downfall, . . . pride.

I am thankful Pastor boldly speaks forth the Word of God. It has kept me anchored thus far. It has kept me reaching for more of the Word. It has changed me. Letter by letter... it is changing me. God spoke this to me too - He is reaching out, He's always reaching out - but I've got to TAKE His hand. And once I take it, **I've got to hold on to Him.** It's my choice. Man or God. Me or Jesus. Flesh or Holy Spirit. Choose ye this day whom ye will serve... I place before you life and death, blessings and curses - CHOOSE LIFE.

i CHOOSE life.

✐ 59**Grow Up!**
(02/27/02 – afternoon radio drive time)

Do you know yourself?
Beloved, I wish above all things that you would prosper and grow up even as your soul prospers – Jeremiah 17:9.
It is so painful, the truth
It sets you free, but it devastates your emotions first
It crucifies your soul

How do you handle temptation?

59

Reach the point where you can be totally honest, truthful and
laying bare before God (and if necessary, others)
Maturity is prosperity and results in integrity
Love corrects – James 1:12.

✐ ⁶⁰What's Wrong? – What's Right?
(03/19/02 – 8:45am)

Life's changes . . . what shall you reap? Issues or blessings
You face life's crossroads - you must decide
Do you make the right choices or the wrong turns
How do you know? . . . Who do you listen to?
Listen . . . Listen oh so carefully
Listen to the One who speaks to you softly
He will never misdirect you . . . He will never lead you wrong
He will always guide you . . . Back to His throne
He keeps you safe . . . He keeps you secure
He keeps you in His arms . . . When your path becomes unsure
His promises are always, "Yes and Amen"
You can depend on His Word . . . To provide the path to a
Friend
So listen
Listen with your spirit
Listen with a clean heart
Listen with a renewed mind

Oh, and yes, there are a couple things you must do first,
Cast down the imaginations of your unregenerate soul
Crucify your flesh and its worldly idols

Then you can be free to let the Anointed One and His Anointing
abound
Flood through your spirit . . . Cleansing your mind
Washing your heart . . . And changing your life
Then you'll know through God's Wisdom, what's wrong and
what's right.

✑ 61Strongholds
(03/19/02 – 11:29am)

Breaking the chains that bind your mind
Breaking the cords that control your life
Freeing your spirit to rule your soul
What are the strongholds keeping you from what's right?
Are they generational curses from your mother?
Are they hereditary curses from your father?
Are you able to see them in the history of your family?
Then, yes, you too can break free.

You see – Jesus Christ already paid the going rate
To set you free and not a moment too late
He has already petitioned the Father on behalf of your case
Saying, "Daddy, my blood was the recompense"

So you are no longer the weakest link
Because that old stronghold is now a broken fence
Satan the strong man, has been defeated by THE MAN Jesus
Christ
And He has taken residence once and for all in your life

61

When you stood in your liberty in Jesus Christ
The Anointed One and His Anointing set you free
There are no more "sacred" closets or hiding places
Satan and his demons have had to flee

Your life is open now and free to all scrutiny
In faith you are declared more than a conqueror
Your righteousness in Christ Jesus is your key
As you stand forever in unity with the Holy Trinity

✎ 62Just Let Go

(03/19/02 – 12:05pm)

How do you hold on?
Just let go
How do you keep what you own?
Just let go
How do you make it right?
Just let go
How do you sacrifice?
Just let go
How do you gain more?
Just let go
How do you let go?
You love.
Love releases you to . . .
Just let go.

62

✐ [63]Rest in Faith
(03/19/02 – 12:07pm)

When we have faith in God, we rest.
When we have faith in man, we wrest.
When we have faith in ourselves, we stress.
When you have faith in Christ Jesus – you rest.

✐ [64]Do The Right Thang
(03/19/02 – 7:41pm)

Learn your lessons early
Don't wait until you're old
Pay what you owe
So you owe nothing but love
Do the right thang

✐ [65]You're On My Mind
(03/20/02 – 6:58am and 03/25/02 – 11:05am)

My Repentance . . .
You're on my mind because I love you
But I hurt you
You're on my mind because I miss you
But I lied to you
You're on my mind because I betrayed you
Yes I disappointed you

63

64

65

You're on my mind because I'm sorry
Will you forgive me?

Your Response . . .
You're on my mind because I love you
So I forgave you
You're on my mind because I made you
Please come back to Me
You're on my mind and I'll never forsake you
Just believe Me
You're on my mind because you are Mine
You're always on my mind

✐ 66Who Am I

(03/20/02 – 7:12am)

Maybe I tried too hard to please you
When I should have been more pleasing to God
Who am I that I should hurt for you now?

Maybe I tried too hard to hold onto you
When I should have been busy chasing after God
Who am I that I should mourn what is lost?

Maybe I tried too hard to know you
When I should have been truly knowing God
Who am I that I should complain?

Maybe I tried too hard to find me in you
When I should have been only seeking God
Who am I that I should die to me?

⁶⁷I Can Only Pray

(03/20/02 – 7:34am)

I messed up
I blew it
I have no excuse
There comes a place where you go beyond sadness
There comes a place where you go beyond pain
You go to a place of numbness
You go to a place of shame

I cannot change what has happened
I cannot change what has been done
I can only pray for healing
For all of my loved ones

I messed up
I blew it
I have no excuse
Yes, I was wrong and I was selfish
Yes, I was faithless and I was blind
I was not following God, instead I was full of me, myself and I
I hurt a lot of people, you being the primary one

I cannot change what has happened
I cannot change what has been done

67

I can only pray for peace of mind
For all of my loved ones

✐ [68]You Let Me Go

(03/20/02 – 8:05am)

You let me go . . . after I broke your heart
You let me go . . . after I broke my word
You let me go . . . after I broke your trust
You let me go . . . after I broke my silence
You let me go . . . after you promised never to let go
You let me go . . . because you're only human

✐ [69]I Wanna Know Love

(03/20/02 – 8:20am)

I wanna know what Love is
Holy Spirit please show me
I wanna know who God is
I know His love is holy
God is Love
Love is God
I wanna know what Love is
Holy Spirit please show me
I wanna know who God is
I know His love is holy
I wanna know God
I wanna know Love

68

69

✐ 70**Dare I Blame You?**

(03/20/02 – 8:30am)

Dare I cast the first stone? Who am I to judge?
Dare I look down at you? Who am I to judge?
Dare I feel cleaner than most men? Who am I to judge?
Dare I blame you? Who am I to judge?

✐ 71**Cast Not Away Your Confidence**
(Hebrews 10:35-37)

(03/20/02 – 9:21am)

Do not be condemned by your heart
Do not be tormented by your sin
For God is greater than our consciousness
And nothing is greater than Him
So cast <u>not</u> away your confidence
Do not let your cockiness be displaced
Know in your heart that you are God's righteousness
Rest in the assurance of your salvation
Rest in the power of His grace
Do not let sin steal your compensation
Look only to Jesus' face

So yes you dropped the ball and missed the mark
You did not exercise your victory in Christ
You messed up and stepped into a pothole of life
Just don't let your confidence be shot
Know that God has already made full provision

70

71

For all of your mistakes
So you don't have to qualify yourself
When you fall from His grace
Just get back up and back in the race
For Jesus Christ has already made recompense
And your latter end has been secured at His expense

Do not fear the devil for he is a defeated foe
Remember, Satan attacks your strength by trying to kill your joy
Let your confidence level be based only in Jesus
Do not be swayed by the demon spirits or what your heart may feel
Know that the key is "cast not away your confidence"
For only in this (holding tight to your assurance in the Word) shall you win!

✐ 72Jesus Loves Me
(03/20/02 – 9:31am)

Jesus loves me
He proves it over and over again
Jesus Christ the same yesterday, today and forever
Even in the midst of my sins
Jesus proves just how much He loves me
His arms remain open wide to gently take me in

Jesus loves me
It is a cry that resounds throughout my heart
He will put me back together

72

When my life is falling apart
You see God knew the mistakes I would make before I was
created
Yet, He did not pause in His commitment to give His life for
mine
Nor did the Messiah consider me useless, and by this I know
Jesus loves me so very much, for my Bible tells me so

He could have tossed me, on the junk pile of life
But instead, for me, Jesus made the ultimate sacrifice
He died and was raised, just to set me free
He came to my rescue, and pulled me out of sin, *in spite of me*
I can never hope to understand the depth of His love
I can only thank God for His Son Jesus up above

Feeling abandoned by your loved ones? – Jesus will never
leave you
Turned friends into enemies? – Jesus sticks closer than a
brother
So when you think you are worthless – God uses broken
vessels
Let God pick you up and turn you around when you feel
down in the dump
Remember only that Jesus loves you . . . Jesus loves you . . .
Jesus . . . Loves . . . You
And God don't make no junk!

✐ [73]The Broken Vessel, the Cracked Pot

(03/20/02 – 10:01am)

Broken vessels don't hold in water to become rank and old
Broken vessels can only spill out the Water of Life upon your thirsty soul
Broken vessels don't hold in air to become puffed up or bold
Broken vessels can only breathe out the Gospel of Jesus Christ to make you whole
Broken vessels don't hold in fire and remain dead cold
Broken vessels can only release the fire of the Holy Ghost and refine you like precious gold

So don't despair if your life seems shot
He takes your offered little and He makes a lot
He plans to use <u>you</u> – the broken vessel, the cracked pot
Not the perfect pottery without a blemish or a spot
So wait patiently on the shelf of the Master Potter until the fire is hot
For God to bless others through you – His broken vessel, His cracked pot.

✐ [74]Slow Down to God's Way

(03/22/02 – 1:20am)

Slow down – you're moving too fast
Only what you do for Christ will last
Don't judge your service by what men will say
For to truly serve God, you've got to slow down to God's way

73

74

113

Slow down – you're moving too fast
Jesus is the Director of life and He chooses the cast
Don't try to pick what role you will play
For to truly serve God, you've got to slow down to God's way

Slow down – you're moving too fast
Jesus died and rose at Calvary to get rid of your past
Don't choose darkness over the light of day
For to truly serve God, you've got to slow down to God's way

Slow down – you're moving too fast
Listen to the Word of God as you knock, seek and ask
Do what it says and true recompense it will pay
For to truly serve God, you've got to slow down to God's way

✐ 75 Deep Inside
(03/22/02 – 1:39am)

Deep inside of me is a Light I can not see
It is a Light that burns bright as it guides me through my
nights
When I close my physical eyes the Light becomes my guide
Like a lamp unto my feet and a Light unto my path
The Light directs me far away from the valley of the shadow
of death

Deep inside of me is a Light I can not see
It is a Light that shines upon the darkest parts of me
When I close my physical eyes the Light becomes my guide

Like an illuminator into my very soul and the mirror to my
heart
The Light lasers to the very root of evil until it and I are torn
apart

Deep inside of me is a Light I can not see
It is a Light that sees the little child I was never allowed to be
When I close my physical eyes the Light becomes my guide
Like a burning bush it calls me to a sacred and holy ground
The Light reveals that only when I trust in Jesus Christ will
I be found
And deep inside of me will His love eternally abound

✐ 76The Covenant Marriage
(Ephesians 5:30-33)
(03/22/02 – 2:12am)

Marriages are not made . . . In heaven
Marriages are not made . . . On earth
Marriages are not made . . . By two
(Two do not make a marriage . . . until they center Jesus
Christ as their holding glue)

Covenant Marriages are not made
Until by two . . . on earth . . . through and in heaven
Agree and say I do
Promising to sacrifice all of me in obedience to only you

76

✐ [77]The Name of Fame
(03/22/02 – 3:35pm)

In whose name will you register fame?
For what price shall you collect the claim?
For the race is not given to the swift or the sure
But to the one in Jesus who is forever secure

In whose name will you register fame?
Will you settle for power, wealth and worldly gain?
When you seek His hand, His face shall He hide
And your search for riches will leave you on a roller coaster ride

In whose name will you register fame?
I would advise Jesus Christ, the name above all names
He is the only One with power to lift up or to raise
His fame is legend and His name is worthy of all praise

✐ [78]Cleansed, Forever Covered by Love
(03/25/02 – 10:41am)

I have been washed and cleansed from within
Jesus and I are in covenant and He removed all my sins
I am cleansed, forever covered by His blood
Jesus has rescued me and I am covered by His love.

I have been washed clean by the blood of Mary's Lamb
Alpha and Omega, the Marvelous I AM

[77]

[78]

I am cleansed, forever covered by His blood
Jesus has rescued me and I am covered by His love.

I am covered not just once as by the blood of bulls and goats
The blood of Jesus is my sure anchor of hope
I am covered not just once a year by atonement
For the blood of Jesus is an eternal testament

Washed in His blood … cleansed forever
Covered by His love
Seated in Christ above … cleansed forever
Covered by His love
Jesus has rescued . . .
Jesus has rescued . . .
Jesus has rescued me!

✐ [79]**Treasure of God's Heart**
(03/25/02 – 10:55am)

Cleansed by Jesus of all earthly lusts
He who dwells in the secret place
Dwells in the treasure of God's heart

Walking by faith in God's mercy and grace
He who dwells in the secret place
Dwells in the treasure of God's heart

---

[79]

⌏ ⁸⁰Forgive Yourself
(03/25/02 – 11:15am)

Forgive yourself . . . unlock the door
For Jesus stands without . . . knocking

Forgive yourself . . . let your yesterday go
For Jesus hung upon the cross . . . saving

Forgive yourself . . . just repent!
For Jesus' blood is forever . . . cleansing

Forgive yourself . . . stand bold in faith
For Jesus sits at the right hand of God . . . reconciling

Forgive yourself . . . receive the Gift
For God gave Jesus just for you.

⌏ ⁸¹Where Your Heart Is . . . Matters
(03/25/02 – 12:45pm)

Where your heart is . . . matters
Is it is the arm of flesh or in God's keeping?
Where your heart is . . . matters
Is it in human strife or in a holy unity?
Where your heart is . . . matters
So, where is your heart?

80

81

✐ ⁸²I Can't Forget

(03/27/02 – 3:45pm)

Dreams come upon the day
Images of you never fade away
I can't forget your love for the right over the wrong
I can't forget . . . you

Laughing out loud while crying inside
Memories surface in my mind
I can't forget the deep and yes, quicksilver responses in your eyes
I can't forget . . . you

Yesterday is gone and tomorrow is sure
The page has turned and our futures are clear and secure
I can't forget the sacrifice Jesus made for all mankind
Lord knows, I can't forget . . . You.

✐ ⁸³Laugh

(03/28/02 – 6:57am)

Laughter never dies for it leaves behind big open smiles
Laughter never dies for it erases pain between close friends
Laugh, for a merry heart doeth good like a medicine

Laughter never dies for it dries the sadness of tears from our eyes

---

82

83

Laughter never dies for it changes our heart and blesses our lives
Laugh, for a merry heart doeth good like a medicine

✐ [84]No Greater Love . . .
(03/28/02 – 7:17am)

What will you give up for a friend?
Will you give up your riches and honor, your glory and your fame?
No greater love than this, that a man would lay down his life for a friend
What will you give up for a friend?

What will you give up for a friend?
Will you walk in the valley of the shadow of death, humbled by shame?
No greater love than this, that a man would lay down his life for a friend
What will you give up for a friend?

What will you give up for a friend?
Will you receive man's reproach and the indictment for all blame?
No greater love than this, that a man would lay down his life for a friend
What will you give up for a friend?

What will you give up for a friend?

84

Will you die to self and renounce all given by birth to your
name?
No greater love than this, that a man would lay down his life
for a friend
What will you give up for a friend?

✎ 85Unconditionally
(03/28/02 – 11:37am)

Does it show, your love for Him, unconditionally?
Will you bow and worship Him only?

Does it show, your love for him, unconditionally?
Will you submit and obey him humbly?

Does it show, your love for her, unconditionally?
Will you discipline and disciple her wisely?

Does it show, your love for them, unconditionally?
Will you let them see Jesus in you daily?

✎ 86Wisdom
(03/28/02 – 11:43am)

How can you learn if you think you know it all?
How can you grow if you think you're grown?
How can you believe God for what you already see?
Choose life and learn all of God's ordinances through Wisdom

85

86

Choose life and grow up through the meat of God's Word
through Wisdom
Choose life and have faith in God enough to seek (early)
Wisdom
Wisdom will cause you to flee all human vice
Wisdom will give you eternal life
Wisdom will reward you with what has no price

✐ 87God is Love

(03/29/02 – 4:54pm)

His glory, for me, He set aside
The angels questioned
"What is man that he is on Your mind"
God answered and called you and me
His Belovéd Child

✐ 88Boundaries

(04/01/02 – 12:21pm)

Boundaries
On my mind
Renewing it daily to the Word of God
Boundaries
On my flesh
No longer shall I focus on me, myself and I
Boundaries
On my emotions

87

88

Forgetting those things behind, I press on towards
the mark of the high calling of Jesus Christ
Boundaries
Will save me from me
Boundaries
Will give me life through Jesus eternally

✐ ⁸⁹Just Leave It In . . . Yesterday

(04/03/02 – 10:36am)

Stop apologizing, . . . forgive yourself
Just leave your regrets in . . . yesterday
Grab hold; . . . refresh your joy
Just leave your sorrows in . . . yesterday
Be blessed; . . . sow seeds of obedience
Just leave your selfishness in . . . yesterday
Be renewed; . . . commit to the Word of God
Just leave your sins in . . . yesterday
It's gone . . . the past is over and tossed in the sea of
forgetfulness
Just leave it in . . . yesterday

✐ ⁹⁰Springtime is here

(04/03/02 – 10:53am)

Smiles abound as joy floods your heart
Minds are renewed by a brand new start

89

90

God's love for you is deep and true
Springtime is here a time to start anew

✒ ⁹¹Canned Emotions
(04/03/02 – 11:12am)

I'm dumping all the preserved feelings
I'm cleaning out the attic of desires
I'm getting rid of all the canned emotions
I'm making room for Jesus Christ
And I'm staying obedient only to God

Starting a fresh and tossing yesterday
No old memories to stand in my way
I'm getting rid of all the canned emotions
I'm welcoming in the Holy Spirit
And I'm staying obedient only to God

✒ ⁹²Today Is My Saturday
(04/03/02 – 3:43pm)

Today is my Saturday
I stand between tragedies of yesterday
I stand between the resurrection of Son day

Today is my Saturday
I vow to stay close to the Lamb of God
I will not run away this time from His love

91

92

124

Today is my Saturday
All the shame of my filth and guilt is in the past
Only what Jesus Christ did on the cross for me will last

Today is my Saturday . . . and I will live.

✐ [93]By His side
(04/05/02 – 12:26pm)

Today I am standing with Jesus, by His side
I am neither standing in front or standing behind
Jesus' footsteps I could never hope to fill
So I stand with Jesus heart in heart, by His side

Today I am standing with Jesus, by His side
I am standing before the Father God unafraid with nothing to hide
Jesus walked in my footsteps on Calvary's hill
So I stand with Jesus heart in heart, by His side

He keeps me near Him
When I feel I am unworthy of His love
He keeps me near Him
When I feel I am unworthy of His grace
He keeps me near Him
When I feel I am unworthy of His mercy
So I stand with Jesus heart in heart, by His side

Why?

93

Because
Jesus loves me – God loves me – the Holy Spirit loves me
Love keeps me inseparably nigh, by His side

✍ ⁹⁴Today
(04/05/02 – 1:07pm)

Today
I thank you for showing me Your ways
Today
I thank you for the debt Your love continually pays
Today
I thank you for Life . . . today

✍ ⁹⁵Alpha & Omega
(04/05/02 – 1:15pm)

**Adonai Lovingly Preserves Humanity Agelessly &
Overcomes Moloch Eternally Glorifying Abba**

✍ ⁹⁶I AM inside of thee (1 Samuel 16:7c; Isaiah 11:3; 30:19; Matthew 7:7,8)
(04/07/02 – 4:25pm)

Seek Me deep inside of men
Look not at their faces but look within
Look for Me and you shall see

94

95

96

I AM inside of thee

If you seek to find My way
My Word you must obey
Look for Me and you shall see
I AM inside of thee

So dry your eyes and cry no more
I hold the key to every locked door
Look for Me and you shall see
I AM inside of thee

My Beloved – seek, knock, only ask
I shall equip you for every task
Look for Me and you shall see
I AM inside of thee

✎ [97]**Prophecy 2 U**
(04/07/02 – 4:35pm)

Last night before ten whilst in quiet time with God, He spoke this into my spirit and my heart. He said, "I have called you and anointed you and appointed you Phasia. I have given you the ministry of song (not singing, but) in poetry to free them from their destruction. Yes, I have cleansed you, so dry your tears and cry no more. Let joy flood your heart and your spirit and as it does it shall wash away all fear and you shall see me, clearly in others. You shall look at them and seek to find me and when you do this you shall see me. You shall obey and come to know my way. Keep your focus on

---

[97]

Me. Yes, I have healed you as I said in Exodus 15:26 – I am the Lord that healeth thee, I am the Lord your healer. So lift up your head and be encouraged with my Strength, for my strength is your joy. Hold fast to it. Let no one take it from you. Learn of Me, the Me on the inside of thee. Walk in that knowledge. Remember I love you. Oh yeah – keep smiling."

✐ ⁹⁸Never . . .
(04/07/02 – 5:05pm)

Never . . . forget My love for you
Never . . . forget you are Mine
Never . . . forget I died for you
Never . . . forget you are on My mind
Never . . . forget Me

✐ ⁹⁹Love Your Neighbor . . .
Galatians 5:14-26 (Rap style)
(04/08/02 – 8:20am)

You gotta love
Gotta love
Love your neighbor
For if you bite and devour one another you're only living in strife
But Jesus came that you not die in the flesh for in Him you shall have life

---

98

99

Homegrown

You gotta love
Gotta love
Love your neighbor
You gotta take care not to be consumed by one another in the
flesh
But I say, walk and live habitually in the Spirit of Holiness

You gotta love
Gotta love
Love your neighbor
For if you oppose the cravings and desires of godless human
nature
You shall be freed from conflict with the Holy Spirit and
deemed mature

You gotta love
Gotta love
Love your neighbor
For the flesh and the Spirit are continually withstanding one
another
You've got to be led by the Holy Spirit of God and none other

You gotta love, gotta love
Gotta love
Love your neighbor

Now here are the doings you've got to avoid
They are works of the flesh that'll try to yank your cord
Immorality, impurity and indecency
Idolatry, sorcery and enmity
Strife, jealousy and anger to get your back up
The enemy keeps tab of what causes you to mess up
Know for sure selfishness, divisions and the party spirit

Team up with envy, drunkenness and carousing to offend the
Holy Spirit
So be warned if you do these works they count as a demerit
And the kingdom of God without repentance you shall not
inherit

You gotta love, gotta love
Gotta love
Love your neighbor

But the fruit of the Spirit and the work of His Presence
Is love, joy, peace and forbearance
Kindness, goodness and faithfulness
Gentleness or humility and self-continence
Against such things there is no law that can bring a charge
For Greater is the One inside of us than he in the world at
large
And those who belong to Christ Jesus have crucified the flesh
Taking up their cross daily they march in line controlled by
holiness

You gotta love
Gotta love
Love your neighbor

So don't be provoked and irritated
Cast down pride, jealousy and be not self-conceited
Be restored in the spirit of meekness and stay in God's favor
Follow his greatest command to love God as you love your
neighbor
God is Love, for to love God is to love yourself
God is Love, as you love your neighbor you dwell in God's
righteousness

You gotta love
Gotta love
Love your neighbor

You gotta love
Gotta love
Love your neighbor

Gotta love
Gotta love
Love your neighbor

✎ [100]Bless Your Holy Name
(04/08/02 – 8:30am)

Hallelujah
Hallelujah
Hallelujah
Hallelujah
Hallelujah
Hallelujah
Bless Your Holy Name
Glory to You
Glory to You
Glory to You
Glory to You
Glory to You
Glory to You
Bless Your Holy Name

100

✎ ¹⁰¹Fighting With Faith, Winning By Love . . . Hebrews 12:1-4 (Rap style)
(04/08/02 – 9:51am)

Glory to God! Glory to God! I'm back on track Lord,
My hand is to the plow and I ain't looking back!
Help me Jesus, keep those ragged emotions in place
I'm running hard with no weights to complete the race

My heart is restored and my trust is in You
My mind is made up and I know what to do

Father God, I know You're on the winning side
Waiting patiently in love for my finishing stride
The saints are cheering me on during those roiling rides
Knowing only by faith will I master life's stormy tides

My heart is restored and my faith is in You
My mind is made up and I know what to do

For the race is not given to the quick, strong or self-assured
Nor to the ones losing heart in the face of life's pressures,
The race is only given to the one who endures
The battles of life knowing the Believers' end is secured

These struggles against sin are only a test
Satan's been defeated and we win <u>if</u> we confess
The Word of God – God's Truth and Light
He will vanquish all our fears and banish our frights

101

So we confess our faith being true to God above
Winning not in strife <u>but</u> only through God's love

✐ 102Exhorted to Win

(04/08/02 – 10:05am)

My Friend, there is no situation too rough or tough for God. Cast it. Just let it go. Put your mind on Him and let it there remain. Of course it's not easy, but it is possible. It is because He promised to never give you more than you could bear. He is with you, inside of you. He is there waiting for you to lean and rest in Him. Go to Him. Curl up in His lap and let Him comfort you. Let God love you like no man or woman ever could, even when we try our hardest. His Love is cleansing and healing and it builds you up always. I love you, but God loves you better.

✐ 103. . . Christ Strengthens You!

(04/08/02 – 11:42am)

There's nothing you can't do
Through Jesus Christ who strengthens you!

✐ 104Holy Tools

(04/08/02 – 1:52pm)

We are all tools

102

103

104

But ask yourself the question
Am I a tool of God available and meet for the Master's use?

We are all tools
But ask yourself the question
Am I a tool of God avoiding strife and works of the flesh that only confuse?

We are all tools
But ask yourself the question
Am I a tool of God open to spread the Word and bring to others the Good News?

We are all tools
But ask yourself the question
Am I or am I not a Holy Tool?

✐ [105]Ephesians 6:12-18 ... Armed to Win!
(04/12/02 – 10:15am)

Stand up and arm yourself to win
Stand up and arm yourself to win
Gird your loins with the Truth
In Christ
<u>You</u> protect your soul from the disease of sin

Stand up and arm yourself to win
Stand up and arm yourself to win
Guard your heart with the Word
In Christ

---

[105]

<u>You</u> prevent death's demons from entering in

Stand up and arm yourself to win
Stand up and arm yourself to win
Shod your feet in the Way and the Light
In Christ
<u>You</u> prepare your life for the Gospel of Peace

Stand up and arm yourself to win
Stand up and arm yourself to win
Garrison your seed of faith with Jesus' victory
In Christ
<u>You</u> shield your mind from Satan's fiery darts of fear

Stand up and arm yourself to win
Stand up and arm yourself to win
Renew your mind, adorn the helmet and repair your story
In Christ
<u>You</u> receive Salvation; His love is yours . . . only persevere

Stand up, fully armed and fight to the end
Stand up, fully armed and fight to the end
Wield the sword of the Spirit and learn how to dominate
In Christ
<u>You</u> battle in prayer and for fellow believers always supplicate

Put up-on purpose the whole armour of God – His Trinity,
Three in One
Stand up against the wiles of the devil for in Jesus Christ you
have already won!

✐ 106**Soul-mates**
(4/16/02 – 8:29am)

From the end back to the beginning
I, God Almighty, shall perform reverse engineering
And your latter end shall be greater than your past
When your soul finds it's mate in Jesus Christ, the First and
the Last

✐ 107**The Battlefield**
(5/6/02 – 1:45pm)

The battlefield is littered with those who gave up the fight
They chose to do the wrong instead of what was right
They did not put on the armor of the Word and were quickly
lost to the night
The choices were placed before them – life and death
Some in the darkness of sin, held fast to the lusts of the flesh
They wouldn't see pass their sins and only felt hopelessness
Alas, their prize is an eternity with Satan and his demons in Hell

Others clung tightly to the Rock of Ages
They sought Wisdom from the Bible's illuminating pages
They were fully armored in the Word, their Christian attire
Living in godliness they reflect the brightness of God' glory
Blinding their enemy and knowing to the victor comes the spoil
The price was their life in exchange for Jesus' righteousness
Amen! Their prize is eternity with the Holy Trinity
Which side are you on?

106

107

✐ 108Go Forth . . . Don't Just Stand

(5/9/02 – 9:00am)

Yesterday, I had this belief or opinion that all I needed to do
was to just stand
But I received a word today from God's Word in Habakkuk
3:19 (Amplified version)

"The Lord God is my Strength, my personal bravery, and my
invincible army; He makes my feet like hind's feet and will
make me to walk [not to stand still in terror, but to walk] and
make [spiritual] progress upon my high places [of trouble,
suffering, or responsibility]!

So I shall move ahead to keep from sliding backwards
I shall keep walking, headed towards God in faith
I won't stop going forth and I won't stand still in terror and fear
I will change my confession and rejoice in the midst of my
trials and troubles
I will grow in Love and gain that precious fruit of the Spirit
called patience

Come let the fire you are walking in refine you and bring out
your true godly character
Take the test rejoicing and praise God boldly and joyfully for
the promotion

108

✐ ¹⁰⁹Incompatible
(5/9/02 – 9:25am)

Some things in life just won't mix
They are just incompatible
Cleanliness and dirt have no common ground
One is upright and the other remains cast down

Some things in life just won't mix
They are just incompatible
Light and darkness won't and can't both surround
One is revealing and the other flees to the outer bounds

Some things in life just won't mix
They are just incompatible
Life and death is not just a state of mind
One restores and the other kills all of its kind

Some things in life just won't mix
They are just incompatible
Don't try to mix and conform to sin
But be ye transformed by God deep within

✐ ¹¹⁰Stop Invading My Mind
(5/14/01 – 6:56am)

Leave me be and stop invading my mind
You are not welcome here you are no longer a friend of mine
Take your words of deception and stay far away from me

109

110

Leave me be and stop invading my mind

Leave me be and stop invading my mind
Get out of my dreams and stay away from my thoughts
Take your acts of rejection and stay far away from me
Leave me be and stop invading my mind

Leave me be and stop invading my mind
Get out of my world and stop messing with my heart
Take your looks of correction and stay far away from me
Leave me be and stop invading my mind

✐ [111]Have You Ever?
(5/14/02 – 7:04am)

Have you ever been so fed up with yourself you didn't quite
know what to do? Have you ever just cried out to God to
just help you through? Have you ever just gotten tired of
what you thought and what you would do? Have you ever?
Have you ever just cried in your heart for the wrongs you
thought? Have you ever just wanted to cry tears of pity and
tears of anger? Have you ever felt like you'd never change
because you didn't see it happening? Have you ever just
trusted God to bring about what you needed when it looked
like you would never be okay? Have you ever just given up
on your way and turned it over to Jesus? Have you ever?
Have you ever just hugged yourself and pressed on through?
Have you ever said Lord, it's yours 'cause I don't know what
else to do? Have you ever not had anyone to call or to listen

---

[111]

to you? Have you ever? Have you ever asked God to help
you please Him first? Have you ever? Have you ever?

✐ [112]Just Keep Living . . .
(5/14/02 – 12pm)

Keep living and your today will become your past
God <u>does not desire</u> that you quit, He has designed you to last
Keep living and your today will become your past
Cry if you must but know the tears will surely pass
Keep living and your today will become your past
Choose life, not death, to pass this life's required test
Keep living and your today will become your past
You may not be perfect <u>yet</u> but just do your best
Keep living and your today will become your past
Listen to the Holy Spirit and godly friends' advice
Keep living and your today will become your past
Stay focused only on the Word and Jesus Christ
Keep living and your today will become your past
Just keep living . . . (for this too shall pass)

✐ [113]Whose Language Are You Talking?
(5/14/02 – 12:45pm)

LOL, Nevermind, 611 . . . whose language are you talking?
Alert Me, Page Me, IM Me . . . whose language are you talking?
(Grin), (Smile), (Squinty eyes) . . . whose language are you
talking?

112

113

Promise, Pledge, Commit . . . (W)hose language are you talking?

Meditate, Listen, Hearken . . . Whose language are you talking?

Study, Read, Hear, Speak . . . Whose language are you talking?

Obey, Follow, Do . . . Whose language are you talking?

Faith, Trust, Blessed . . . Whose language are you talking?

Worship, Deliver, Praise . . . Whose language are you talking?

Just <u>whose</u> language are you talking?

✎ 114Defraud Not God, Cheating Yourself . . . Expect Sumpthin!
1 Corinthians 6,7; 1 Thessalonians 4 & Philippians 1:19,20
(5/15/02 – Amplified Version 10:27am & 5/24/02 – 10:25am)

Stop vacillating back and forth in your heart

Make up your mind Baby Girl (Baby Boy)

Are you walking on the Word or not?

What are you expecting to happen in your life?

Are you seeking the victory? Or worse . . . Are you looking for the defeat?

(Shake yo'self Baby Girl . . . Baby Boy! Huh! Get down wit'yo funky self!)

Don't allow the right moment of opportunity to pass you by!

Pick up your God-given tools from the Word and keep fighting against sin

You gotta expect "sumpthin" good to make it in victory to the end

Have great expectation 'cause through Christ Jesus you're sure to win

---

114

✎ 115A Thousand Pardons

(5/25/02 – 10:38am)

Giggles, captured in the hearts of four and the faces of two
A woman covered with God's spirit of wisdom, teaching youths
Denetra
Tears, captured in the face and the heart of one
A woman covered with God's beauty for ashes, reaping love
Denetra
Peace, captured in the glory and presence of God
A woman covered with God's favor and grace, seeking joy
Denetra
I would give a thousand prayers to see again your smile
Denetra
I would ask a thousand pardons to turn back the pain of time
Denetra
I would say a thousand apologies to witness God's laughter in your eyes

✎ 116Driven to . . . God

(5/30/02 – 6:45am)

Why are you mad at what you are going through?
Don't you know you are being perfected through your trials?
Come let yourself be transformed into Christ's image
Come let yourself be driven to . . . God

Why are you trying to run away from what you are becoming?

115

116

Don't you know you must pass through this wilderness?
Come let yourself be transformed into Christ's image
Come let yourself be driven to . . . God

Why are you still looking for approval from mankind?
Don't you know you must lean and trust only in the Word?
Come let yourself be transformed into Christ's image
Come let yourself be driven to . . . God

Why are you so concerned about your popularity and
reputation?
Don't you know you must cast off the old in order to put on
the new?
Come let yourself be transformed into Christ's image
Come let yourself be driven to . . . God

Why are you so bitter about changing into someone better?
Don't you know you are being shaped into His spiritual
creation?
Come let yourself be transformed into Christ's image
Come let yourself be driven to . . . God

✎ 117. . . Beyond Hope

(5/30/02 – 2:15pm)

Have you ever gotten beyond hope . . . and
just believed the Word of God?
Have you ever gotten beyond hope . . .
and just prayed the Word of God?

117

Have you ever gotten beyond hope . . . and
just declared the Word of God?
Have you ever gotten beyond hope . . . and
just stood on the Word of God?
Are you still hoping for the manifestation of your future?
Or is it as real to you as though you have it right now?
God says . . . stretch forth your faith and
belief . . . beyond hope to just receiving
God says . . . get out beyond hope to
celebrating in its completion!
God says . . . get out beyond hope to victory for you win!

✎ [118]So You Want A Miracle?

(6/9/02 – 1:01am)

My husband . . . my covering
I am so glad you finally stopped being so self-less
I am so glad you stopped allowing me to be so selfish
You have taken your stand
Truly you are God's man
I love you . . . not just with my words
Let me show you, my lord . . . by my actions

So you want a miracle? Are you willing to
drink of the cup offered to the obedient?
Come and sup with Me . . . take of My Word and drink deeply
The miracles don't come to the ordinary . . . but to
the ones willing to be tested and found true
Come let Me make of you a miracle . . . come
let Me make a new creation of you

My Lord . . . my Covering
I am so glad You planted your seed deep inside of me
I am so glad You took root and grew
and are even now bearing fruit
I have humbled myself . . . my will to You
I have submitted and become a woman of Virtue
I love You . . . not just with my words
Let me show you, my Lord . . . by my life

✐ 119Intimately Knowing You God

(6/11/02 – 3:30pm)

I want to know You intimately . . .
Becoming so knowledgeable of Your
Word that I see Your way clearly
I want to know You intimately . . .
Becoming so aligned to Your Spirit
that I walk boldly without fear
I want to know You intimately . . .
Becoming so attuned to Your voice
that I obey without question
I want to know You intimately . . .
Becoming so identical to You that
others hear You when I speak
I want to know You intimately . . .
Becoming so inseparably one with You that
through me others feel Your love deeply
I want to know You intimately . . .
Just as You . . . God . . . know me

120Looking At My Life Today . . . (smile)
(6/11/02 – 7:50pm)

My life has taken many twists and turns over the
last several months . . . over the past few years
There were sharp turns where all I could do was
hold on tightly for fear of losing grip on life
Sometimes the turns meandered and were
winding as though leading to nowhere
I have advanced in my relationships with God,
my husband (and daughter) and myself
I have confidence again (or maybe for the first
time) and an assurance my life shall bring
forth a recompense of great reward
I am walking some days, running others and some days
I find myself even crawling through the Word . . .
In all of this, I am learning (even now) that God is with me
Some days (and nights) I feel like I haven't
gained any ground and I'm still where I started
out with just more mistakes than victories
Other days (and nights) I feel exhilarated and
excited about where I'm headed with faith
that I am a dominator and not a victim
I have discovered during this period that
I have the strength of a godly husband to lean upon
I have the wisdom of God to call upon
I have the honesty of godly friends to
encourage, correct and exhort me
And I have the Word of God to chastise,
change and mature me

I am being transformed into who I need to be
and each moment is one of fresh victory
I am less than I thought myself to be . . . and
hopefully more of whom God desires me to be
Strength is certainly made perfect in weakness . . .
His Strength and my weakness
I am shored up by His love in all my areas
of lack for He knows my heart
Thank you Lord.
I am impressed by His patience when I
was so disobedient and rebellious
Thank you Father.
I am humbled by His forgiveness of all
my sinful thoughts and actions
Thank you Jesus.
I am comforted by His peace when I
face challenges and tribulations
Thank you Holy Spirit.
Your Joy gives me strength to persevere
Your Anointing gives me power to overcome
Your Word gives me the right to dominate
I am more prosperous . . . I am more blessed . . .
I am more favored . . . in the sight of God
I am His child
Looking at my life today . . . I'm not where
I need to be . . . but I'm on my way.
Thank God . . . I'm on my way (smile).

✑ 121A Mirror To Your Soul

(6/20/02 – 3:35pm)

Hiding . . . behind a façade of smiles
Your pain you try to camouflage
Suppressing . . . the Holy Spirit
While you cry inside
Come out of concealment . . . life is <u>not</u> 'let's make a deal'
No more masquerades . . . God knows your hurts are real
Look and you shall clearly see
The Truth . . . instead of deceit
His Word . . . a mirror to your soul
To unmask your mind and make you whole
Look into God's Truth . . . and find the mirror to your soul

✑ 122The Me You Want Me To Be

(6/20/02 – 4:14pm)

Do you really want me . . . do you really want to know me?
Or do you only want to know the 'me' you want me to be?
Do you really love me . . . do you really want to love me?
Or do you only want to love the 'me' you want me to be?
Have patience . . .
Only God can change me into the 'me' you want me to be.

121

122

148

✎ 123Daddy… Abba, Help Me To Find Your Way

(6/21/02 – 12:06am)

Dreams come at the close of the day
Chasing the nightmare of my thoughts far away
I seek to be in Your will O Lord
Help me find Your way

Afraid to look at what I may see
Images of the past all around me
I seek to know Your purpose O Lord
Help me find Your way

Invisible bonds keeping me close yet far
Near enough to touch yet miles from where you are
I seek to walk in Your footsteps O Lord
Help me find Your way

Visions of what might have been
Reality of what is gone for sin
I seek to feel Your heart O Lord
Help me find Your way

Laughing out loud while crying inside
My heart from You I cannot hide
I seek to see Your light O Lord
Help me find Your way

✐ 124His (. . . Anointing)

(6/21/02 – 12:16am)

Beautiful music
Words of worship to you
A musician of note
Godly and so full of Truth
Filled with Your wisdom
Anointed to give You praise
Healing the broken-hearted
Raising men from the dead

Keys of poignancy
Accompany words of love
Given Your clean heart
To offer back to You up above
Singing soul-filled melodies
Phrases manifesting Your promise
Stirring up the faith of others
And giving to You a lifetime of homage

Plucking at the life strings
Of every believer's heart
Telling of a faithful promise
Telling of a brand new start
Walking in the miracle
You have designed him to be
A man on a mission
A man fulfilling – to You – his destiny

124

✐ ¹²⁵No Time For Games

(6/21/02 – 7:42am)

Be real
Life is short
No time for games
Renew your heart

Be open
Walk in love
No time for games
Seek God above

Be true
Faith comes by hearing
No time for games
The Word is conscious searing

There is no time for games

✐ ¹²⁶Selfishness Unveiled

(6/24/02 – 6:38am)

God is Holiness . . . His Love never fails
Before His Presence . . . man's selfishness is unveiled

125

126

✎ 127Natural and Spiritual
(7/2/02 – 3:01pm)

There is a natural side and a spiritual side to each of us
In the natural . . . we see things we really
don't see and are easily deceived
In the spiritual . . . seeing the light of God's
Truth we can more clearly perceive
In the natural . . . before people . . . we can easily
fool others and put up a smoke screen
In the spiritual . . . before God . . . we can hide
nothing in darkness for in His eyes <u>all</u> is seen
In the natural . . . we're operating blindly
in the flesh and are weak
In the spirit . . . God's anointing is
upon us to make us complete
I am a spirit who has a soul – my mind, will
and emotions – and I live in a body
I am a spirit learning – by walking in the Spirit –
how to dominate the natural side of me

✎ 128Peace with God
(7/22/02 – 3:15pm)

Peace with God . . . through icy rains of despair
and disappointment ripping through my life
Peace with God . . . in the smothering
darkness of boredom cloaking my mind

127

128

Peace with God . . . during roller-coaster
changes that upsets all preconceived plans
Peace with God . . . when all is well and the
normalcy of life is like a never-ending story
God has given me peace . . . a calmness that fills my mind
God has given me peace . . . a stillness that quiets my heart
God has given me peace . . . a richness that colors my life
God has given me peace . . . a satisfaction
that satiates my soul
God has given me peace . . . a promise
that He shall always keep

✐ 129A Covenant God

(8/2/02 – 3:15pm)

His name is I AM Jealous . . . and He is my God
He will not leave me . . . if . . . I humble myself to His way
He expects me to cast down Satan's
devices for they shall not prosper
He expects me not to covet what is not mine
thereby opening up a doorway for sin
Forget how I FEEL . . . just walk in His will
God is a covenant God . . . He is not man that He should lie
And whatever I have need of . . . I
know El Shaddai shall supply

129

✎ [130]**Remembering August 6**
(8/5/02 – 9:35pm & 8/6/02 – 3:00pm)

Remembering August 6
Remembering the birth of a friend
Called to remember my purpose
And a friendship that had to end
Born to exalt God and living to worship His name
Celebrating life as I hearken obediently to His plan
Staying focused on God only . . . and not on man

Remembering August 6
Remembering when my life began
Called to remember my covenant . . .
Marriage comes first over any other friendship
Winning the battle over the thoughts of my mind
Knowing that my life is in a new season
And the devil comes back to tempt . . . just for this reason

Remembering August 6
Tossing down the gauntlet of the Word
As I wave high the flag of victory
Giving praise **now** expecting my supernatural miracles
As God's fresh anointing continues to flow my way
My weaknesses are made strong in His power and liberty
Remembering August 6 . . . the day
I **decided** to become free

✎ 131Beauty for Ashes

(8/9/02 – 6:38am)

Cremate the ashes of your past in the
consuming fire of God's Holiness
And toss those ashes far away into His sea of forgetfulness
We cannot have our ashes and God's beauty too
Must give up the one in exchange for being made new
Get rid of what's dead so you may live renewed
For the fresh and the new Anointing is waiting for you

✎ 132God's Plan . . . God's Purpose

(8/20/02 – 5:58pm)

God has a purpose in mind for me
A perfect plan that ~ for now ~ I cannot clearly see
So I will hearken and I'll obey Him instantly
Because God designed me to walk only in victory

God is depositing words of Wisdom into my memory
When I walk in His Word I'm released from flesh's slavery
So I spend quiet time in the pages of biblical history
And I reap the rewards of God's spiritual nobility

131

132

🖋 133Obedience is (so much) better than sacrifice
(9/13/02 – 7:48pm)

God says do you love Me . . . if so, what will
you sacrifice to prove your obedience?
Will you withhold your life and throw
away salvation's perfect Sacrifice?
Will you idolize work or worldly pursuits
over God's heavenly Substitute?
God says do you love Me . . . if so, can you count the ways?
Will you hold onto your ministry and forget
you were sent to bring others?
Will you let go of your best and allow
God to anoint it until it's blessed?
God says do you love Me . . . if so, what
will you give so <u>you</u> will know?
Obedience is (so much) better than sacrifice.

🖋 134Postage Stamps on the Letter of Life
(9/15/02 – 7:29am)

(All of our) Goals and plans are but
postage stamps on the letter of life.

133

134

✐ ¹³⁵Wisdom Whispers Across My Mind
(9/23/02 – 7:56pm)

Like an impression that leads to reflection
Wisdom whispers across my mind
Words spoken softly . . . in mine ear
Words of edification . . . for my heart to hear
Like an impression that leads to reflection
Wisdom whispers across my mind

✐ ¹³⁶Never Alone (Psalms 23)
(10/19/02 – 11:30am)

Never Alone
He promised not to leave me on my own
Never Alone
He draws me ever nearer to His throne

And though my heart's uncertain
I search to find my way
He makes the path of righteousness
Straight when I obey

He leads me by the gentle streams
I have peace to hear His Voice
He shows me the right paths to take
When I'm faced with a choice

Never Alone

135

136

He promised not to leave me on my own
Never Alone
He draws me ever nearer to His throne

You've prepared a rich feast for me
My cup overflows
In your Presence I desire to be
'Cause only there do I know

Your Word lights my pathway
Showing my feet the way to go
You alone are my pilot
I'm blessed with supernatural overflow

I'm Never Alone
You promise not to leave me on my own
Never Alone
Your Love has drawn me close to Your throne

I'm never alone . . . (Thank you Jesus)

✒ 137 10-20-LIFE (Psalms 91)

(10/28/02 – 5:23am)

10-20-Life
That's what the world gives to you
But my Father gives Life more abundantly

10-20-Life

Describes the world's finite love for you

But my Father forgives and forgets all your iniquity

10-20-Life

Will keep you locked up 'til kingdom come

But my Father has set you up in eternity

with His only-begotten Son

10-20-Life

Don't take the crap

Let God be your Judge as Jesus Christ beats the rap

✐ ¹³⁸Love (1 Peter 4:7,8)

(11/10/02 – 4:01pm)

The end of all things is near

Therefore be self-controlled and make your mind clear

Pray!

And watch closely the words that you say.

God commands you to love and love deeply one another

For through God's love, will a multitude of sins He cover

Love!

For this is God the Father's will from heaven above.

The end of all things is near

Therefore be self-controlled and make your mind clear

138

✐ [139]Heart-kisses Upon My Soul (Psalms 119:105)

(11/10/02 – 5:22pm)

God's Word brings heart kisses upon my soul
His Word is a lamp showing me which way to go
Gentle flutters of love upon my heart
His Word leads me to the light away from the dark

God's Word brings heart kisses upon my soul
His Truth guides me straight to His perfect goal
Gentle flutters of love upon my heart
His Word leads me to the light away from the dark

God's Word brings heart kisses upon my soul
His Word is a light showing me the right road
Gentle flutters of love upon my heart
His Word leads me to the light away from the dark

---

[139]

Printed in the United States
By Bookmasters